CONTENTS

Chapter Five : HOUSING CONDITIONS

Chapter Six : COMMUNITY ISSUES

£10.70

UTH IN MAPS

Economic Atlas

D. J. Maguire

M. Brayshay

S. Chalkley

of Geographical Sciences

outh Polytechnic

1987

PREFACE

This atlas provides a portfolio of maps, some computer-drawn and some drawn by cartographers, which, together with the supporting commentary, offer a portrait of Plymouth in the 1980s. Our endeavours in "putting Plymouth on the map" are intended to be of interest to a wide readership. For teachers and lecturers, including those bringing field parties to Plymouth, the atlas should prove a rich source of material for work in geography, local history, environmental science and social studies. Local policy-makers and various professional, voluntary and amenity groups should also find the atlas a source of insight and information. Above all, we hope that our work will be of interest to those who it is principally about – namely the people of Plymouth.

The maps utilize a wide range of data sources but the most important are first, the 1981 Population Census, and, secondly a series of specially-commissioned surveys undertaken by a team of Manpower Services Commission survey workers. The Census data are presented mainly in the form of ward-level maps (**Fig. 1** shows the ward names and boundaries), but in order to underline the degree of intra-ward variability, some maps have been included at the finer geographical scale of the enumeration district. Although no Census maps are included showing trends between 1971 and 1981 (boundary revisions make such comparisons difficult) readers interested in changes over time will find it helpful to consult a previous social atlas of Plymouth which used 1971 data and was produced by Dr Ken Dean of the College of St Mark and St John, Plymouth. The MSC work for the present atlas was designed to obtain information on themes not addressed by the Census. A major household survey, with some 3000 interviews, was conducted in clusters of enumeration districts selected to be representative of the city as a whole. The areas chosen are shown in **Fig. 2** (obviously their boundaries do not coincide precisely with the areas to which particular local place names apply and the place names used are therefore for indicative purposes only). Smaller surveys were undertaken on tourism and on the public's appraisal of Plymouth's central area. The information gathered by the MSC team has also been extensively used outside the atlas for other research programmes and for a wide variety of teaching purposes.

It has therefore provided a multi-purpose information store which will be a resource of lasting value. Further details on the Census and MSC data sources and on the compilation of the maps is contained in the Technical Appendix. The census data set out in the Appendix are reproduced with the permission of the controller of Her Majesty's Stationery Office. (Crown Copyright).

ACKNOWLEDGEMENTS

The authors would like to thank Plymouth Polytechnic, the Manpower Services Commission (MSC), the Elmgrant Trust (at Dartington) and Plymouth City Council for their generous sponsorship of this atlas. We are also grateful to the team of MSC assistants for their work in gathering relevant information: the team comprised Viv Pointon (Supervisor), Simon Durkin, Keith Lewis, Philip Louch, Anthony O'Reilly, Adam Rope, Michelle Skidmore, Deborah Stride, Laura Trevelion, Ian Willey and Tony Quickenden. Allan Jones of the Polytechnic's Geographical Sciences Department also helped to manage the MSC survey workers.

Colleagues in the Polytechnic Business School, in the Department of Social and Political Studies and in the Computer Centre provided a variety of useful information and special thanks are due to Paul Bishop, Joan Chandler, David Dunkerley and also to Colin Rallings who provided much of the material for the section on Plymouth's politics. Various departments of Plymouth City Council helped with information on housing, social services, town planning, environmental health and local election results. Crime statistics were made available by the Crime Prevention Support Unit of the Devon and Cornwall Constabulary. Roger Punch of Oats Partridge provided helpful comments on the city's housing market. We are also grateful to Alison Crabtree for her work in experimenting with the design of the computer-drawn maps and to Rachel Harley and Cathy Howells for typing the manuscript. Steve Johnson of the Polytechnic Media Services Unit provided the photographs. Very special thanks are due to Brian Rogers and Jennifer Wyatt (departmental cartographers) whose expertise is on display in many parts of the atlas.

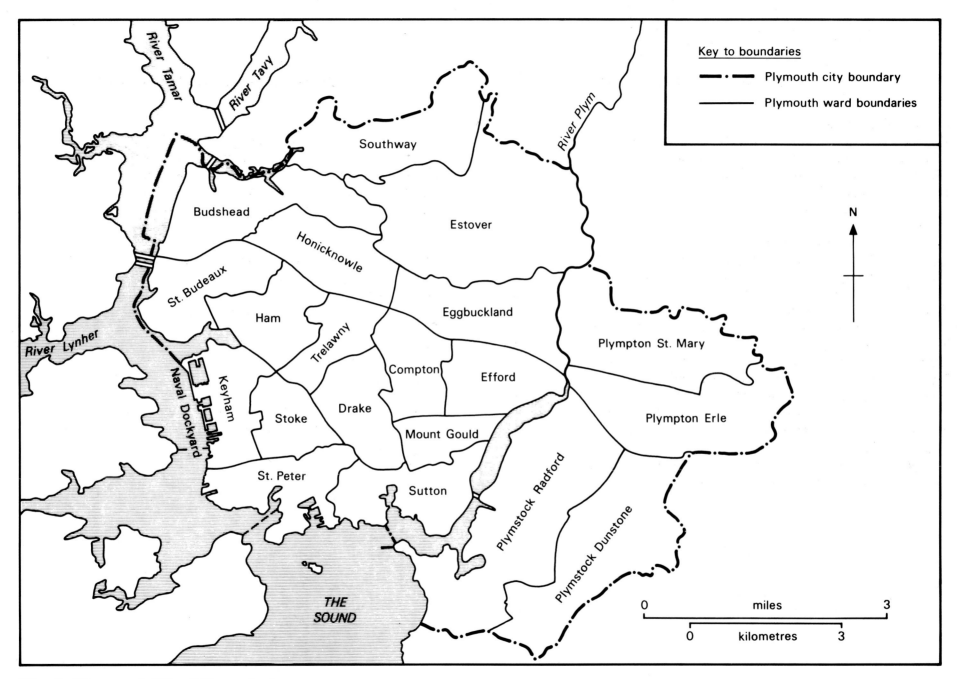

Fig. 1. Plymouth Ward Boundaries.

5

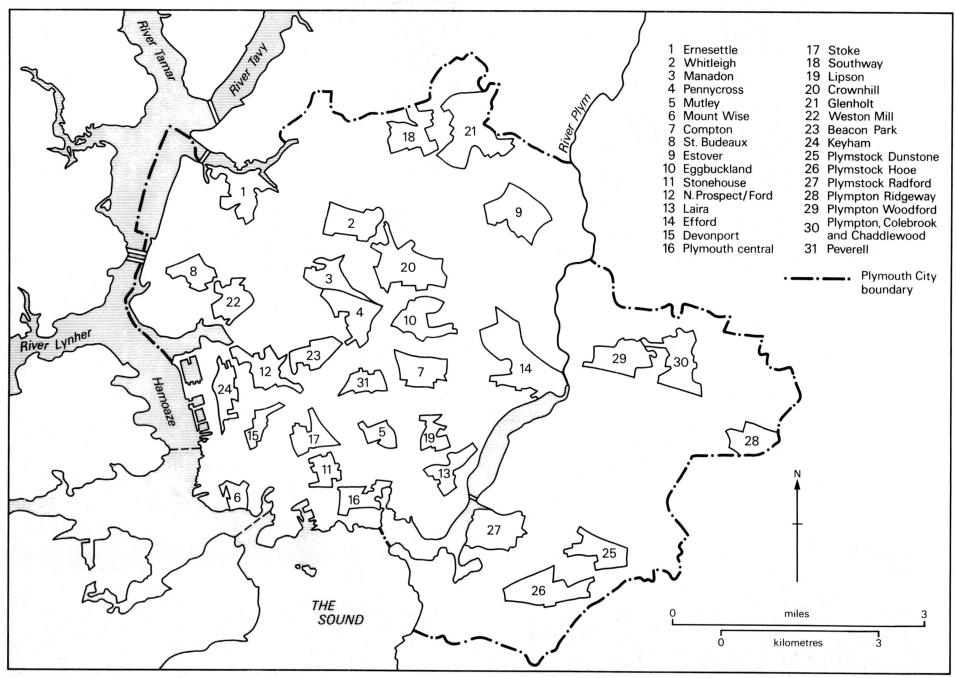

1 Ernesettle
2 Whitleigh
3 Manadon
4 Pennycross
5 Mutley
6 Mount Wise
7 Compton
8 St. Budeaux
9 Estover
10 Eggbuckland
11 Stonehouse
12 N. Prospect/Ford
13 Laira
14 Efford
15 Devonport
16 Plymouth central

17 Stoke
18 Southway
19 Lipson
20 Crownhill
21 Glenholt
22 Weston Mill
23 Beacon Park
24 Keyham
25 Plymstock Dunstone
26 Plymstock Hooe
27 Plymstock Radford
28 Plympton Ridgeway
29 Plympton Woodford
30 Plympton, Colebrook and Chaddlewood
31 Peverell

─ ・ ─ ・ ─   Plymouth City boundary

Fig. 2. Areas of the City Sampled in the Household Survey.

6

One
**Introducing
Plymouth**

Plymouth and its Region

Plymouth is the most remote urban centre in England and Wales. Located in the extreme south-west corner of Devon (see **Fig. 3,** inset) it is 120 miles from Bristol and 225 miles from London. No other provincial city is further removed from a neighbouring centre of comparable or larger size. In the past this degree of geographical isolation has imposed serious problems of communication: Plymouth was once linked to the rest of England by a road described as "the longest lane in England", the A38. Now there is dual carriageway to Exeter and the motorway network beyond to Bristol, London and the Midlands. The rail journey to the Metropolis takes only three hours and the Brymon Airways service from Heathrow to Plymouth takes a mere 60 minutes. Even so, the facts of geography cannot be entirely disregarded and Plymouth remains a uniquely peripheral city whose distance from the national centres of industry and commerce is still an obstacle to economic development.

More positively, the absence of nearby urban rivals has enabled Plymouth to become the undisputed regional service centre for the far south west. Located aside the River Tamar on the boundary between Devon and Cornwall, Plymouth is approximately mid-way between the two county towns of Exeter and Truro (see Fig. 3): although they are the centres of county-level administration, Plymouth has a larger population (245,520 in 1981) than both of them combined. Even the major tourist resort of Torbay is less than half Plymouth's size. As the principal regional service centre, Plymouth offers the largest shopping facilities west of Bristol and a wide range of cultural, leisure and educational facilities. Its theatres, its museum and art galleries, its Polytechnic and Colleges and the presence of the main regional studios for both BBC and commercial television – all illustrate the extent of Plymouth's regional role.

Plymouth's urban status dates back to the year 1254 when its first market charter was received. Thereafter, the natural harbourage afforded by Plymouth Sound enabled the town gradually to emerge as the guardian of the Western Approaches and by the reign of Elizabeth I, it was the most important naval seaport in England. In the 1690's William III decided to build a naval dockyard on undeveloped land flanking the eastern bank of the Tamar, two miles from Plymouth. Today the local economy remains heavily dependent on the Royal Naval Dockyard which now extends over 330 acres and is the city's largest single employer. Although recent years have seen major investment in the frigate refit complex and the nuclear submarine base, the threat of large-scale redundancies currently hangs over the dockyard as part of the government's privatisation proposals. The navy is in retreat and Plymouth's place in history seems a good deal more secure than its prospects for the future. The city's long dependence on the dockyard led Pevsner in his book 'The Buildings of England' to note that Plymouth "is the only British city whose existence appears centred on war".

Britain's victories and defeats at sea have indeed long had a special local significance. But whereas such conflicts have normally been centred on events and places far away, in the Second World War Plymouth itself was in the front line. The German air raids of 1941 produced extraordinary scenes of devastation and the city's central area was literally flattened. The post-war reconstruction programme was guided by a comprehensive plan published in 1943 and prepared jointly by Sir Patrick Abercrombie, the eminent town planner, and Hugh Paton-Watson, Plymouth's city engineer. Their ideas not only re-fashioned the main shopping area, but set in train a major programme of rehousing and population decentralisation. As a result of continued progress in reducing overcrowding and in building new homes, Plymouth now faces a serious land shortage. The city is enclosed by Dartmoor to the north, the Tamar to the west and the Sound to the south. The surrounding areas are politically as well as environmentally sensitive. Neighbouring local authorities are wary of Plymouth's territorial ambitions and the possibility of boundary extensions. Although substantial parts of both counties depend on Plymouth for employment and services and could therefore be said to form part of the Plymouth region, this atlas and the maps it contains are focussed on the more limited area of the 31 square miles within the city boundaries.

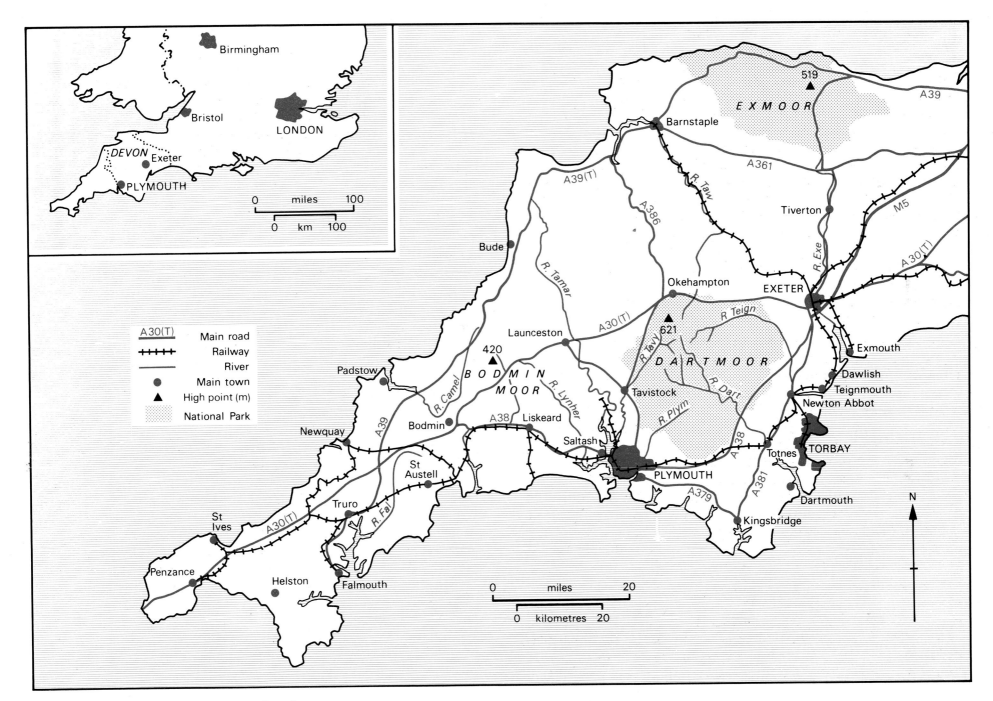

Fig. 3. Plymouth's Regional Setting.

9

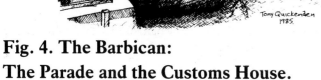

Fig. 4. The Barbican:
The Parade and the Customs House.

The Barbican area is the city's main historic quarter and with its stock of old maritime buildings and its Elizabethan street pattern it provides a landscape link with the past. This sketch of the Customs House Quay was drawn by Tony Quickenden (employed as a member of the Manpower Services Commission Team), and shows a familiar scene in the heart of old Plymouth. The Barbican was the first Conservation Area to be designated in Plymouth (and only the second in the country): here strict planning controls and a programme of landscape enhancement have sought to protect the environment. Many of the area's buildings, including the Customs House (completed in 1820), also enjoy the additional protection of being "listed" as buildings of special historic and architectural interest.

Fig. 5. The Tamar Bridges.

This sketch, also drawn by Tony Quickendon, shows one of Plymouth's best known views, namely the two bridges which span the River Tamar and which in linking Plymouth to Saltash also connect the two counties of Devon and Cornwall. The rail bridge, built in 1859, was designed by Isambard Kingdom Brunel. The road bridge, completed in 1961, has effectively enhanced Plymouth's role as the regional centre and has opened up Saltash and adjacent parts of south-east Cornwall as commuter territory.

Physical Geography

Fig. 6 (overleaf) shows that most of Plymouth, with the exception of the eastern suburbs of Plympton and Plymstock, lies on undulating land between the Tamar (Hamoaze) and Plym valleys which drain south into the fine natural harbour of Plymouth Sound. The southern edge of the land between the two rivers is marked by the limestone ridge known as The Hoe which affords magnificient views across The Sound and out towards the breakwater. The Tamar and Plym estuaries are examples of drowned valleys or rias which were produced by the post-glacial (Flandrian) rise in sea level: such valleys are a distinctive feature of the coastal scenery of the area.

The main topographic feature of the city itself, as shown in Fig. 6, is the central ridge which runs north from Mannamead through Crownhill and rises steadily to the city's northern edge where it leads to the landscapes of Dartmoor. Throughout much of Plymouth, the rocks are Upper Devonian slates known locally as shillet which to the north give way to the more resistant granite uplands of Dartmoor.

Plymouth's climate is portrayed in the histograms in Fig. 6 which are based on data for the period 1974 - 1984. The whole of south west England is noted for its mild maritime climate and Plymouth is no exception. These conditions are a product of the southerly latitude and the area's exposure to the Atlantic westerly air-streams. It is, however, also a region with above average rainfall. Plymouth has a mean annual rainfall of 1000mm and inland towns at higher altitudes are wetter still, the figures for Tavistock and Princetown being 1500mm and 2200mm respectively.

Land Use

The spatial pattern of land use within the city, which is outlined in **Fig. 7** (overleaf), is in part a response to physical and topographic constraints. Plymouth's growth has proceeded northwards over a series of hills. The flatter land of the valley bottoms and hill tops has generally been used for housing and industry whereas some of the steeper slopes have precluded development altogether. A number of coastal creeks have been reclaimed in order to obtain more flat land for building and for playing fields.

It is the city's coastal location and the fact that it could obviously not grow southwards from its original nucleus which account for the non-central location of the city centre (a key feature of the town's everday life). After the destruction brought by the German air raids there was talk of moving the main shopping and civic facilities to a more central location such as Milehouse, but in practice they were rebuilt on their old site, which the city's post-war expansion has made still more geographically eccentric.

Another distinctive feature of land use in Plymouth as revealed in Fig. 7 is the significance of naval and other defence-related uses. The Royal Dockyard at Devonport stretches for three miles along the Hamoaze and there are several other Ministry of Defence sites within the city used principally for barracks, residential, administrative and training purposes.

Housing is, of course, much the largest land use in the city. Generally the newer stock is in the suburban locations, although many of these have grown around older previously separate settlements. For example, Plymouth's two eastern suburbs of Plympton and Plymstock were incorporated into the city by the boundary extension of 1967. The eastern and northern suburbs also contain much of the city's industrial land commonly in the form of post-war industrial estates.

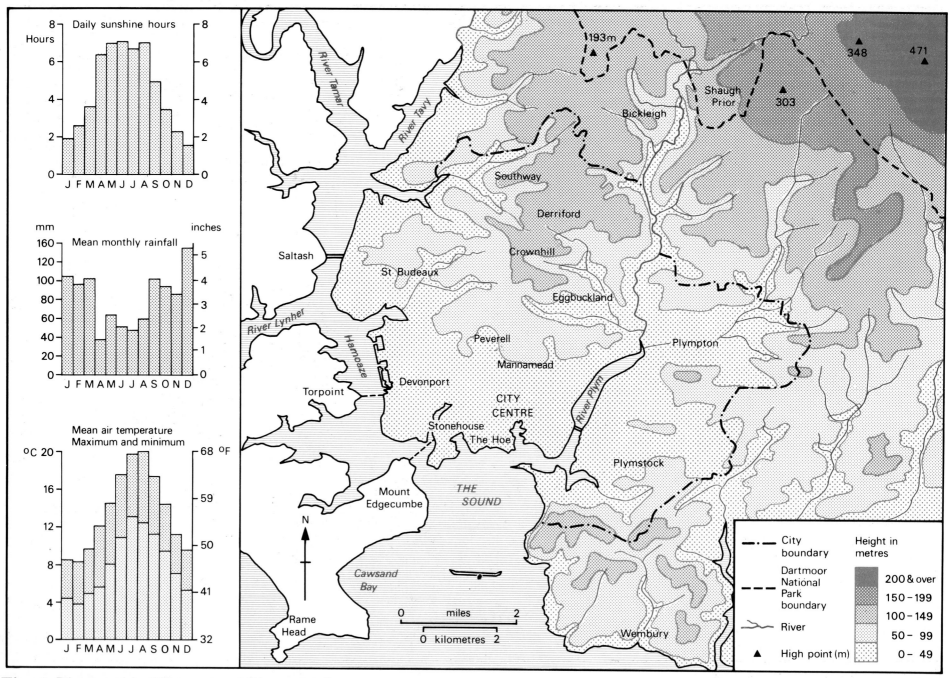

Fig. 6. Plymouth's Climate and Topography.

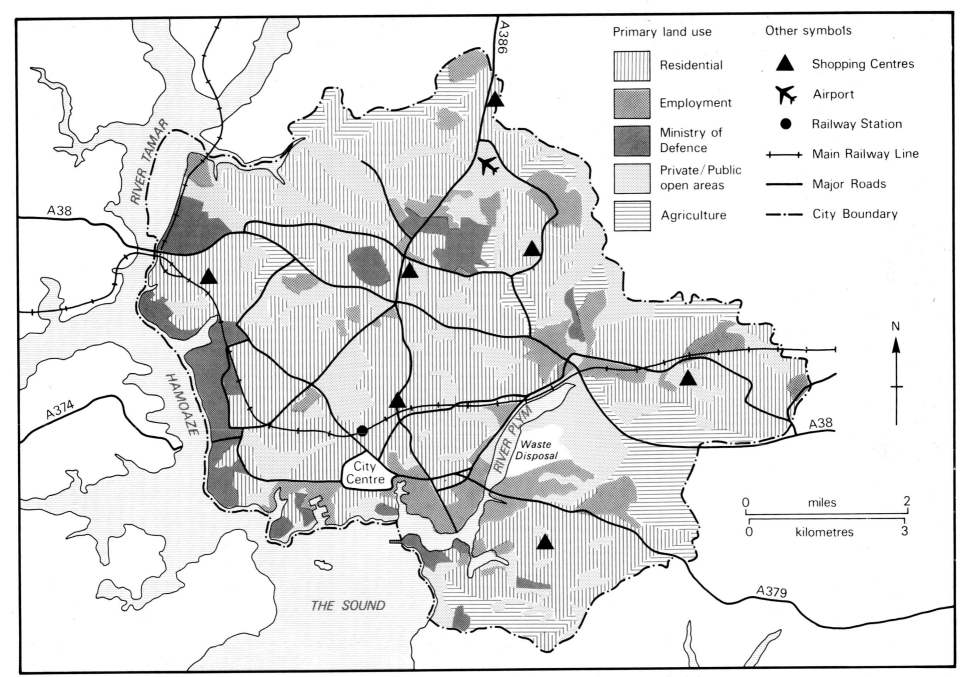

Fig. 7. Land Use in Plymouth.

13

War-time Destruction and the 1943 Plan for Plymouth

When war broke out in 1939 the threat of an air attack was not taken seriously in Plymouth as the city lay beyond the assumed reach of enemy bombers. But this complacency was short lived. Following the fall of France and the chaos of Dunkirk, the city and its naval dockyard were suddenly front-line targets. Altogether Plymouth had 59 raids resulting in 1180 deaths and 3270 injuries to the civilian population (figures for service personnel have never been published). The fiercest raids were on the nights of 20th and 21st March, 1941, when the Luftwaffe caused an estimated £100,000,000 worth of damage (perhaps £1½ - £2 billion at today's values). As **Fig. 8** shows, by the end of the war no district in the city remained unscathed although fortunately the Elizabethan quarter around Southside Street in the Barbican escaped the very worst damage. (In examining the map, note that no data are available on the bombing pattern in the dockyard).

In addition to the human casualties and physical destruction, evacuation and out-migration resulted in a serious drop in population – a matter of real concern in a city so dependent on the distributive trades. Moreover, the bombing deprived the civic treasury of one-third of its rate revenue and there was soon a risk of insolvency. Only a special government subsidy sustained Plymouth through this financial crisis. Even while the raids continued, the city authorities appreciated the need to restore morale by publishing proposals to rebuild and rehabilitate the city as quickly as possible. And well before the end of the war a reconstruction Plan for Plymouth had been devised and agreed in broad principle.

The scale of the destruction presented a unique opportunity to remedy some of Plymouth's pre-war problems, including poor housing, traffic congestion and insufficient open space. Before 1939 there had been only minimal progress in correcting some of these defects chiefly because of the weakness of the planning system. Plymouth had the worst traffic congestion record of any provincial city in southern England. Open space in the central area was 50 per cent below the amount then deemed necessary for a city of Plymouth's size, while housing densities and overcrowding were worse than in Liverpool and parts of London's East End.

Viscount Astor, the city's wartime Lord Mayor, was prominent amongst those who saw a chance to develop in Plymouth an entirely modern concept of a city; he was determined that reconstruction should be 'no half-and-half affair'. At his personal invitation in the summer of 1941, Professor (later Sir) Patrick Abercrombie was engaged as the consultant on the Plan for Plymouth. Abercrombie was professor of town planning at London University and had already been retained to work on reconstruction plans for the capital. But Astor wanted the most eminent authority possible to tackle Plymouth's rebuilding and not for the first time his personal knowledge of people in high places proved decisive. He invited Abercrombie to visit Plymouth and two years later in September 1943 the remarkable Plan for Plymouth was ready. Abercrombie and Plymouth City Engineer, James Paton-Watson, were the co-authors. In spite of some opposition, when the Plan was made public it aroused enormous interest; copies went all over the world, while at home the City Council quickly gave it their approval.

The Plan was deliberately comprehensive in its approach and there were innovative and far-reaching proposals on housing, retailing, employment, communications, population distribution and recreation. However, the two principal elements in the Plan were the new suburban neighbourhood units and the re-design of the city centre. Both these policies have had a profound impact on the post-war geography of the city and are considered in more detail in the sections which follow.

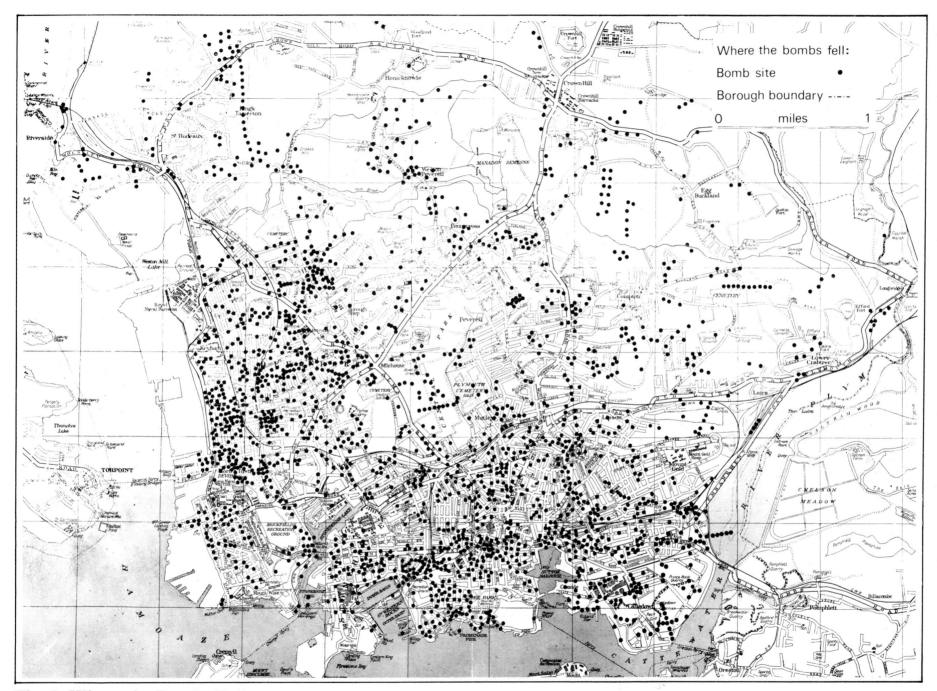

Fig. 8. Where the Bombs Fell.

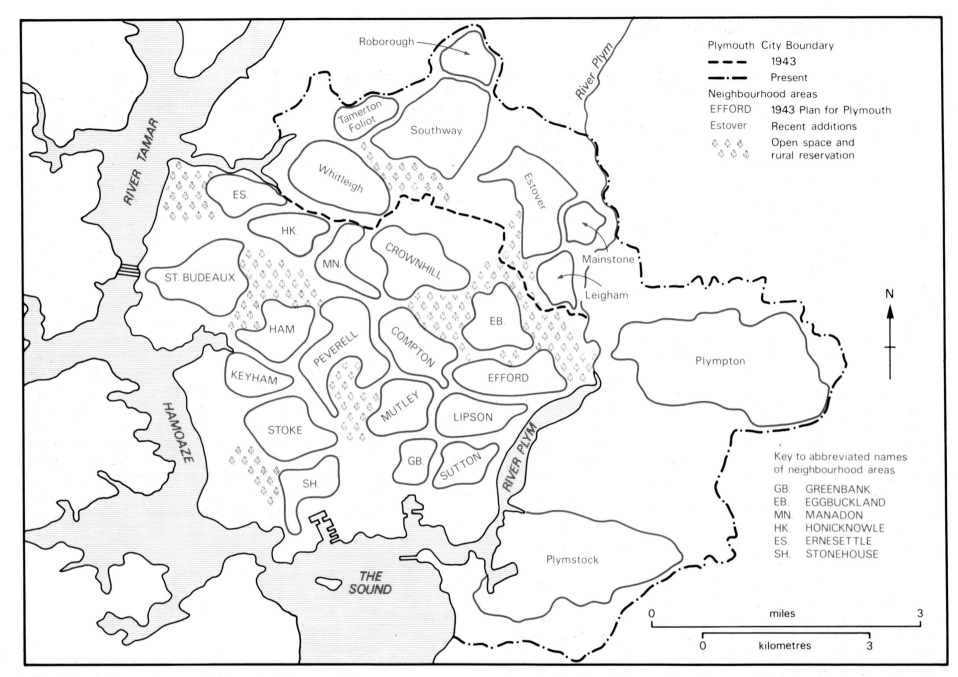

Fig. 9. The Post War Neighbourhood Units.

The Neighbourhood Units

The housing policies of the 1943 Plan were heavily influenced by the ideas and ideals of neighbourhood unit planning and as a result Plymouth today provides some interesting examples of residential areas designed according to neighbourhood unit principles. This approach was very much in fashion in the 1940s and 50s and Abercrombie was one of its most committed adherents. The theory of the neighbourhood unit derived from the view that people live best in small communities and that many of the social and psychological problems characteristic of modern society stem from the anonymity of city life. If urban areas could be broken down into a series of smaller, more village-like communities, each with its own separate identity, a new social cohesion would result. The theory rested on a nostaglia for traditional rural lifestyles: indeed each of the new neighbourhood units in the 1943 Plymouth Plan was to have at its centre a village green (together with community facilities such as shops and public buildings).

Fig. 9 shows Abercrombie's intended divison of Plymouth into neighbourhood units, together with later areas of housing expansion on the city's northern and eastern perimeter as at Southway, Estover, Plympton and Plymstock. Abercrombie himself envisaged five new purpose-built neighbourhood units and another 13 which were to crystalize within the existing built-up area. Abercrombie did concede that within the existing city the theory's implementation would be "somewhat more complex" but nonetheless it still represented the "policy to be aimed at". In practice, radically re-shaping the inherited urban morphology was an unattainable goal and in these areas the policy was never seriously applied. In contrast, in the new housing estates built soon after the war, theory became practice and Abercrombie's ideas were, to a considerable degree, implemented in neighbourhoods like Whitleigh, Honicknowle, Efford and Weston Mill (Fig. 9).

The first neighbourhood unit was in fact started at Efford in December 1945. Thereafter development tended generally to proceed in layers outwards from the existing built-up area, this northwards movement being facilitated by a city boundary extension in 1951. In the early years, the rate of progress was dependent upon building licenses and the availability of material supplies. Nonetheless, by 1955 over 11,000 new dwellings had been added to Plymouth's housing stock and by 1964 the figure had reached 20,000. The neighbourhood units made a major contribution to the city's post-war house building programme and to the associated improvement in Plymouth's housing conditions. Priority in housing allocation was given to families whose homes had been destroyed in the blitz and to those living in the worst of the older slums.

The homes provided in the neighbourhood units were typically three-bedroomed council houses built at densities of between 10 and 12 to the acre and often grouped into short terraces (see photograph top right, page 53). In terms of architecture, landscape and aesthetics, these early estates could not be described as especially imaginative or memorable: topographic constraints and the need for economy and speed took their toll. Nonetheless, in terms of physical standards they were a considerable improvement on the slums of the inner city and, in their level of planning, they represented a clear advance over the unco-ordinated sprawl of the 1930s. Socially, the hoped-for reconstruction of a village community spirit inevitably proved somewhat elusive. Neighbourhoods could not be produced to order or engineered by environmental design, particularly in a period when rising car ownership reduced people's dependence on their home locality and neighbours. Even so, the estates have gradually developed some sense of identity and have become for many residents the subject of personal attachments. Although when judged with hindsight Plymouth's neighbourhood units are inevitably a somewhat qualified success, they do bear testimony to a striking experiment in urban design and one conceived at a particularly bleak and unpromising time in the city's history.

Fig. 10, re-drawn from the 1943 Plan, illustrates Abercrombie's determination that the new neighbourhbood units should be more than simply housing estates: they were to have a full range of facilities and services. In addition to a shopping centre, there was to be a variety of public buildings whose use would help to provide a sense of community and fellowship. In the words of the Plan "today the loss of community spirit is largely due to a lack of conveniently sited meeting places". It was clearly the authors' belief that by physical planning and environmental design, it was possible to manufacture socially effective communities. The central village green symbolises the desired return to the fraternal lifestyles which were thought to characterize traditional rural societies.

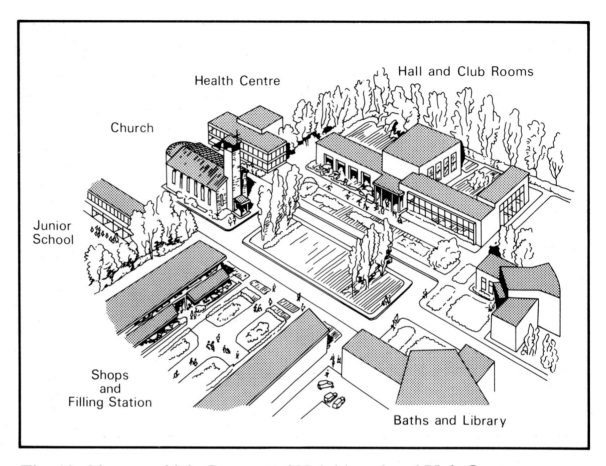

Fig. 10. Abercrombie's Concept of Neighbourhood Unit Centres.

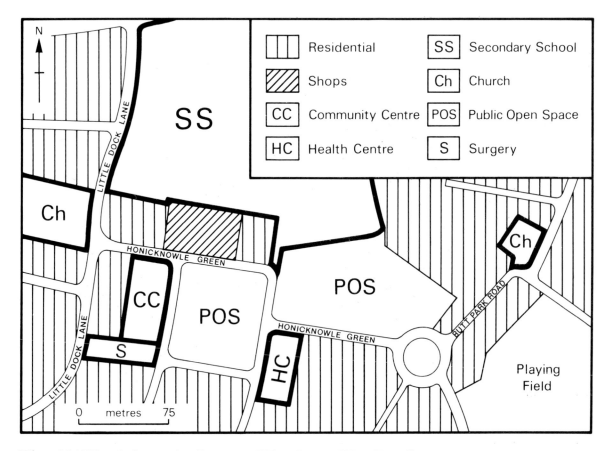

Legend:

Residential			SS	Secondary School
Shops			Ch	Church
CC	Community Centre		POS	Public Open Space
HC	Health Centre		S	Surgery

Fig. 11. Honicknowle Centre: The Post-War Reality.

Fig. 11 presents a simplified current land-use map of Honicknowle's central area and illustrates how far Abercrombie's proposals were put into practice in one of the northern post-war neighbourhood units. The public open space (village green) is surrounded by the shops, community centre, school and health centre which the Plan had envisaged. However, some of Abercrombie's more ambitious ideas, such as the library and public swimming baths, were victims of the need for economy. Moreover, in recent years, school provision in several of the neighbourhood units has encountered the problem of demographic changes and falling rolls leading to a number of closures. In Honicknowle, as elsewhere, it has proved difficult to reconcile the benefits of neighbourhood-based educational provision with the need for a wider rationalization of schooling across the city.

The City Centre Rebuilding

The new city centre was intended as the showpiece of the 1943 Plan. It was to symbolize the re-birth of the city and to provide a shopping and civic environment of which residents could be proud. The blitz had completely destroyed the old central area and many businesses had closed or moved out to Mutley Plain or other parts of the city. In seeking to accommodate and encourage the essential resurgence of city centre retailing, Abercrombie and Paton-Watson envisaged a formal, neo-classical pattern of buildings and townscape whose grandeur and symmetry would bear witness to the advantages of comprehensive planning over piecemeal redevelopment. The splendour of the new city would hold out the promise to beleagured Plymothians of a better tomorrow and, in time, provide some compensation for the sufferings of the war. Abercrombie's proposals were therefore radical, bold and comprehensive. Just how radical is demonstrated in **Fig. 12** which compares the pre and post-war street patterns. The old complicated tangle of streets was literally wiped off the map. Whereas in mainland Europe many of the destroyed cities were rebuilt to their original design, in Plymouth (as elsewhere in Britain) a cleansweep approach was adopted. Abercrombie, to all intents and purposes, embarked on building a new town on a virgin site rather than rebuilding an ancient city.

The post-war street system, which for the most part follows the 1943 Plan, is both simple and geometrical. Whereas many elements of the complex pre-war pattern survive around the edges of the downtown area, the city centre itself has a strikingly clear geometry. The east-west streets in the grid-iron, such as Royal Parade and New George Street, are crossed by the main north-south axis of Armada Way which was intended to forge a wide processional avenue connecting the station (to the north of North Cross Roundabout) with the war memorial on The Hoe. Abercrombie described Armada Way as the Plan's "one great decorative – even monumental – feature". It provides a 1,000 yard vista which was intended to allow visitors and tourists arriving by train an immediate view across the city to the famous Plymouth Hoe. In Abercrombie's words, "they will know where they are".

The new pattern also owes much to its authors' desire to avoid the serious traffic congestion which had choked the pre-war city. An inner ring-road system (using Western Approach, Cobourg Street and Charles Street) was intended to direct 'through' traffic around the edge of the city centre. Within the main shopping area the streets were deliberately built wide to encourage easy traffic flow. The Plan pre-dated the notion of pedestrian-only shopping areas and so the principal shopping streets include busy dual carriageways. It is interesting that more recent retail developments at Drake Circus and in the Armada Centre (at the north end of Armada Way) are pedestrian-only and detailed proposals are currently being implemented for pedestrianising large parts of the city centre. A survey by the Manpower Services Commission team suggests that over 60 percent of those shopping in the central area support the idea of extending pedestrianisation in Plymouth.

In essence therefore, the 1943 Plan aimed for an open, spacious, modern centre with wide boulevards, long vistas and a formal townscape and architecture. The Plan was unveiled on 25th April 1944, and despite some opposition, was approved in principle by the local authority on 4th September 1944. The council then turned to the task of implementation and began the work of acquiring the land, clearing it, providing new roads and services and finally leasing the sites either to companies who built and occupied their own property or to developers who leased the buildings to tenants. The new centre's first kerbstone was laid on 17th March 1947 in Raleigh Street (near Derry's Cross). By the mid 1950s Royal Parade and New George Street were almost complete and development then progressed northward into Cornwall Street. By the mid 1960s most of Abercrombie's proposals had been translated from words and sketches into buildings and townscape.

There were, of course, some significant departures from the Plan. For example, Royal Parade was built narrower than proposed, the memorial ruin of Charles Church was not intended to be imprisoned as the centrepiece of a busy traffic roundabout and the civic centre was not envisaged as a 14 storey tower block.

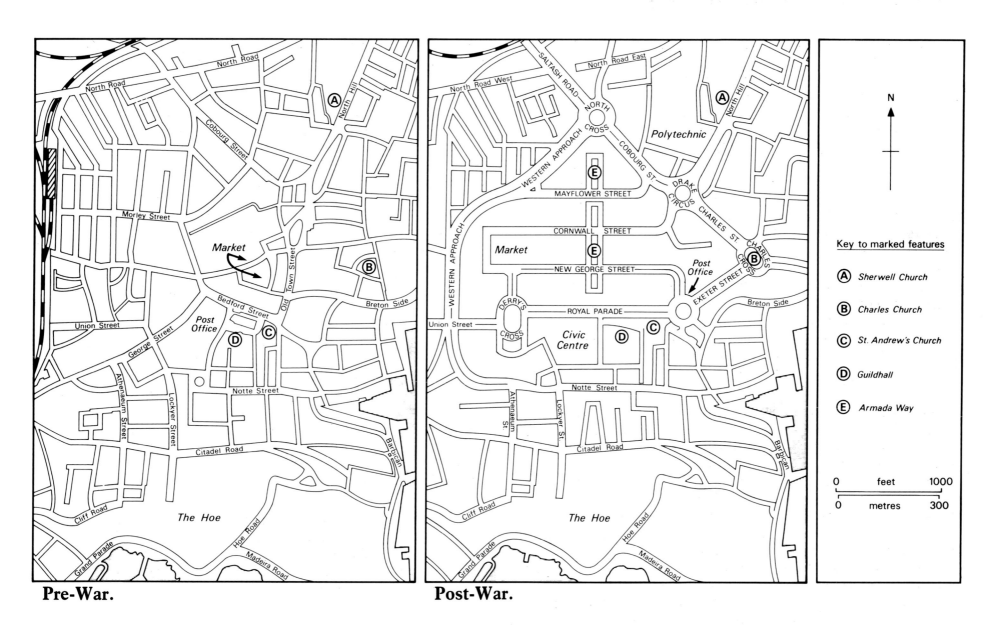

Pre-War.

Post-War.

Key to marked features

(A) Sherwell Church

(B) Charles Church

(C) St. Andrew's Church

(D) Guildhall

(E) Armada Way

Fig. 12. The Central Area Street Patterns.

Another interesting measure of the extent to which the Plan was put into practice is provided by the schematic land-use maps in **Fig. 13** (p.23). Abercrombie envisaged a clear system of land-use zoning and special precincts were to be set aside for uses such as civic buildings, hotels and offices. This segretation of activities is certainly evident in today's system of land-use (albeit Fig. 13b repeats the format of the original Plan and is a much simplified and generalised model of the present pattern). It is interesting that one of the deviations from the Plan, the absence of the Millbay Rotunda, will soon be made good by the provision of a leisure complex in this area. Today's clear separation of land uses into distinct zones has in practice been maintained partly through the council's estate management powers as landlord. This point has in recent years taken on new significance because, unlike many other cities, Plymouth has been able to prevent the intrusion of banks, buildings societies and estate agents into the main shopping streets.

Opinion on the merits of Plymouth's post-war centre are obviously varied. The standard criticism is that the architecture has proved disappointing: the general uniformity of building heights and the Portland stone facades have perhaps given a rather heavy and monotonous appearance to the buildings. Nonetheless, in the MSC survey of people shopping or walking through the down-town area, the proportions considering the buildings attractive and unattractive were approximately equal. It was interesting that tourists and visitors were usually more impressed than local residents and many non-locals remarked on the spacious avenues and general openess and greenery of the city.

One criticism often made by architects and expert commentators is that the central area is deficient in landmarks and reference points. The long straight streets leave little scope for surprise or excitement in the landscape. Because many of the streets look alike, they lack individual identity. This absence of 'legibility' can cause confusion. In this context it is interesting that the MSC survey, which used 10 different interview points along the main city centre streets, found that in total over 40 per cent of the Plymothians questioned were unable to name correctly the street in which they were interviewed. One might have thought it difficult to produce a townscape which could lack both mystery and clarity but in Plymouth this "double negative" has apparently been achieved. This theme of urban anonymity is reinforced by the fact that less than 20 per cent of Plymothians interviewed could name the designer(s) of the post-war city centre. Many local people, it seems, know little of their city's history and the story of its reconstruction. Today's city centre is the legacy of men whose deeds survive in bricks and mortar long after their names have been forgotten.

On a more positive note, it must be emphasized that the post-war city centre has certainly succeeded commercially in reinstating Plymouth as the region's leading retail centre. The level of shopping provision is highly regarded and over 80 per cent of our survey respondents rated the city centre's shops and services as 'good' or 'very good'. Perhaps overall, if one considers the central area rebuilding as a kind of urban heart transplant, we should conclude that the patient has survived, recovered and is successfully back at work but not looking as well as one would have liked.

In order to improve and enliven the city's rather bland appearance, the local authority has recently announced proposals for a major facelift for the city centre streets. The ideas are contained in a brochure called "Tomorrow's Plymouth". In addition to pedestrianisation there are plans for roofing-in some of the streets under curving glass canopies. A new open air market is envisaged and Armada Way is to be re-landscaped and to have fountains and cascades. The recently completed Armada Centre with its luxury hotel, Sainsbury's store and elegant shopping mall may therefore be only the first instalment in a much wider programme of modernisation. We are seeing the first signs that the ideas of the 1940s will need to be re-shaped to meet the needs of the 1990s.

(a) As Proposed by Abercrombie.

(b) Simplified Model of Present Pattern.

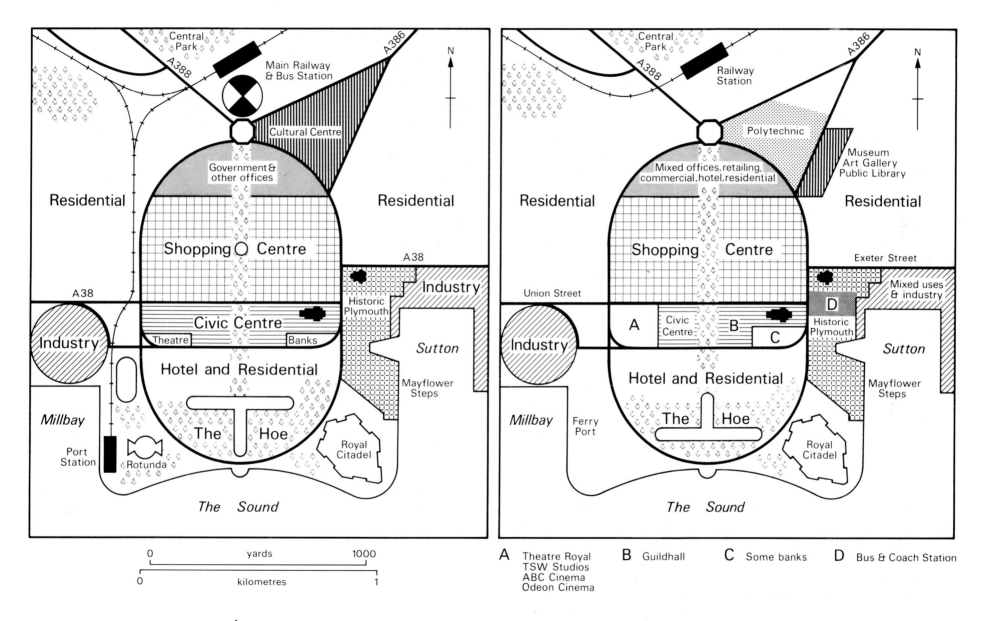

A Theatre Royal
   TSW Studios
   ABC Cinema
   Odeon Cinema

B Guildhall

C Some banks

D Bus & Coach Station

Fig. 13. The Central Area Land Use Zones.

Two
Plymouth's Population

Plymouth's Population

The 1981 Census recorded Plymouth's enumerated population (all persons present on census night) as 245,520. The city's general trend across the century has been one of growth and the only serious downturn came with the war-time evacuation which lowered the population to about 130,000, a reduction of one third. However, numbers were quickly restored after the war and, with the help of boundary extensions in 1951 (for the neighbourhood units) and in 1967 (to take in Plympton and Plymstock) the population rose to 239,400 in 1971. The city's continued growth since then has been modest but is of particular interest in that it is very much at variance with national urban trends. Plymouth is the only one of the country's twenty largest cities which has not experienced a fall in numbers since the 1971 Census. Particularly in Britain's older and larger urban centres a rapid loss of jobs and poor environmental conditions have resulted in a pattern of exodus from which Plymouth has apparently been immune. Although Census data for the city are notoriously difficult to interpret (because of the impact of Armed Services households) it is quite clear that the general tide of urban decline has not reached Plymouth. Given that the city's birth and death rates are not far from the national average, the key differential would seem to be the relatively low level of net out-migration (400 between 1971 and 1981). This may reflect both the attractions of the city's environmental setting and the state of the local economy, which though far from healthy is more buoyant than many metropolitan centres. Moreover, the city is part-surrounded by river, sea and moor and has neighbouring local authorities reluctant to accommodate overspill population; for these reasons Plymouth is less vulnerable than many other cities to population loss through sprawling outward expansion beyond its official boundaries.

In addition to national urban comparisons, it is also of interest to compare Plymouth's demographic characteristics with those of other parts of Devon. Once again, Plymouth is anomolous. It has a much younger age structure than other parts of Devon and, as a result, during the 1971-81 period it was the only one of the county's ten Districts to experience more births than deaths. It was also the only District where more people moved out than moved in (albeit as explained earlier the city's net outflow was small). Both these demographic differences derive in part from the fact that Plymouth has not shared in the large-scale retirement migration which has affected many other parts of Devon, especially around Torbay and Exmouth.

Within Plymouth itself there are, of course, considerable variations in demographic characteristics and trends. For example, the inner-city wards with their rows of terraced housing generally have much higher residential densities than those at the periphery where more spacious layouts are more usual. As explained in chapter one, the local authority has throughout most of the post-war period actively pursued a policy of reducing densities and overcrowding in the inner city by moving people out to new estates on the city's edge. This has obviously led to a re-distribution of population and although no map is presented here of 1971-81 population changes (several ward boundary adjustments make such temporal contrasts difficult), there is no doubt that the general trend towards dispersal has continued.

This centre-versus-periphery theme and the related contrasts between old and new housing areas affect many facets of the city's population geography. For example, the post-war suburban housing estates have attracted a high proportion of young married couples, and especially where housing provision has been both large-scale and rapid (as in Abercrombie's neighbourhood units) the effect has been to produce a 'bulge' in the age structure which over the years has gradually moved upwards through the age groups. By contrast, new entrants to the inner city have been mainly young but single: this has re-inforced the concentration of single-person households in the inner city, a pattern which relates to the supply of flats and 'bed-sit' accommodation.

This theme of geographical contrasts between the older and newer areas is further illustrated in the maps which follow. Most of these focus on the city's age profile, a key element of the city's population geography and one which has considerable implications for public expenditure particularly on social and medical services.

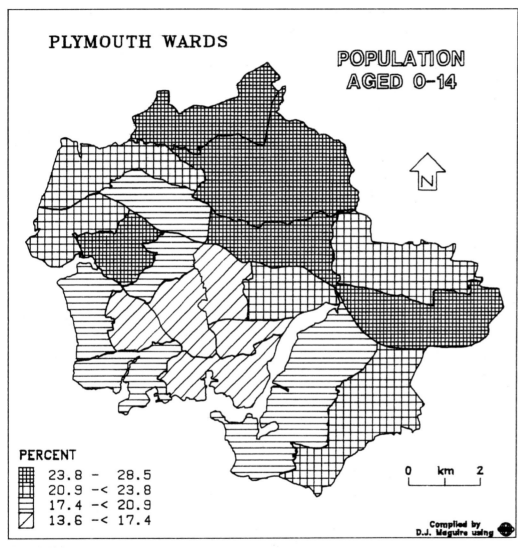

PLYMOUTH WARDS

POPULATION
AGED 0-14

N

PERCENT
23.8 - 28.5
20.9 -< 23.8
17.4 -< 20.9
13.6 -< 17.4

0   km   2

Compiled by
D.J. Maguire using

Fig. 14. Population Aged 0-14 years.

The 1981 Census recorded that 20.6 per cent of Plymouth's population were in the 0-14 age group, but, as **Fig. 14** shows, this overall proportion disguises some striking geographical variations. The highest percentage, 28.5% in the rapidly developing area of Estover, is more than twice that of the inner city ward of Drake which with 13.6 per cent has the lowest figure. Generally it is the suburban areas with their modern family-sized dwellings which have the highest percentages in this youngest age bracket. Families with young children are especially well represented in the newest estates on the city's northern and eastern perimeters. The only western ward in the highest group is Ham which is dominated by council estates including part of the pre-war North Prospect development. Some of the early post-war neighbourhood units (as in Honicknowle and Budshead wards) are now well past their peak in terms of numbers of children and have begun therefore to face the problems of school closure. Even so they still retain a higher proportion of children than the inner city wards. (Readers unfamiliar with Plymouth's ward names will find it helpful to refer back to the ward map on page 5).

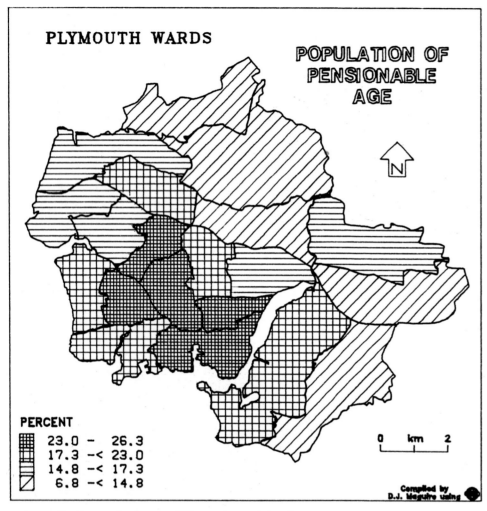

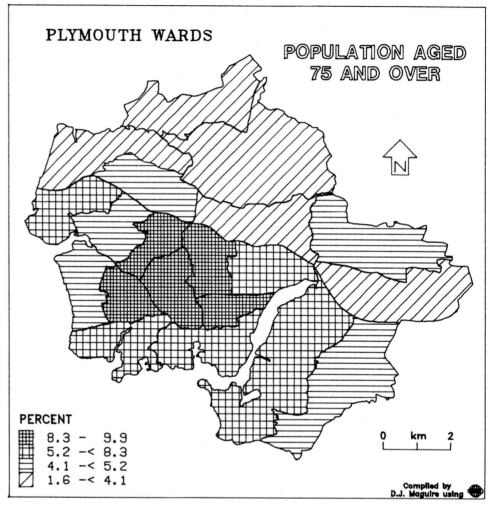

Fig. 15. Population of Pensionable Age.

Fig. 16. Population Aged 75 Years and Over.

Although Plymouth attracts relatively few retirement migrants it has nonetheless shared in the national trend towards an ageing population. Whereas the city's total population grew by only 2.5 per cent during the 1971-81 period, its population of pensionable age increased by 8.65 per cent from 38,405 to 42,018. **Figs. 15** and **16** show that the pensionable population in general, and those aged 75 and over in particular tend to occupy the inner urban areas. The elderly have clearly been unwilling or unable to join the general exodus to the suburbs.

Some Census data are available at the scale of Enumeration Districts which generally contain about 200 households. The two Enumeration District maps, **Fig. 17a** and **b,** show the age structure of the southern (inner city) part of Drake Ward on either side of North Hill. They introduce a finer scale of analysis and point to a feature of particular interest: Britain's inner cities tend to have a 'dual' age structure with high proportions of both the elderly and of young adults attracted by 'bed-sit' accommodation and private-rented housing. The maps indeed show that in this part of Drake Ward these two very different age groups with highly contrasting needs, values and lifestyles live virtually side by side in the same localities.

(a) Persons aged 16-24 years
(b) Persons of retirement age (percentage)

▨	30·0-39·9
▨	20·0-29·9
▨	10·0-19·9
▨	0·0- 9·9

Fig. 17. Age Structure in the Inner City: Drake Ward (South).

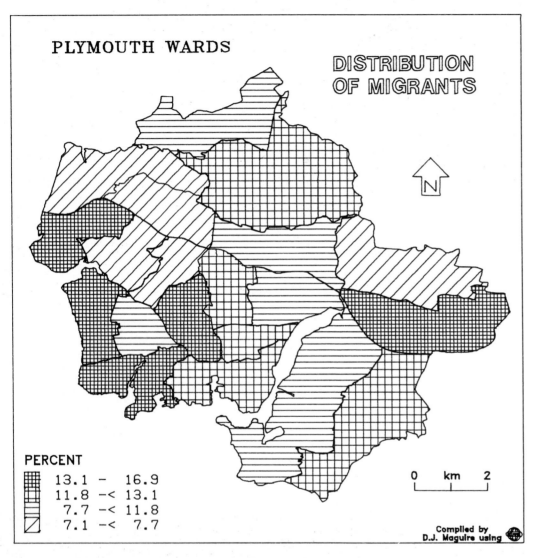

PLYMOUTH WARDS

DISTRIBUTION OF MIGRANTS

N

PERCENT
- 13.1 – 16.9
- 11.8 –< 13.1
- 7.7 –< 11.8
- 7.1 –< 7.7

0   km   2

Compiled by
D.J. Maguire using

Fig. 18. The Distribution of Migrants.

Another significant aspect of the city's population geography is the number and distribution of migrants. The census defines a migrant as someone who on census night has a usual address different from their usual address twelve months earlier. On this basis 11.1 per cent of the city's population were migrants. This is above the national average presumably because of the high mobility among H.M. Services.

The geography of Plymouth's migrants is shown in **Fig. 18.** The contrast between city wards is such that the highest percentage, 16.9 for St Peter, is more than double that for Honicknowle, 7.1. Although new housing completions in the months prior to the census will obviously have inflated the figures for some suburban wards, generally the migrants were concentrated in St Peter, St Budeaux, Keyham and other parts of the inner city. The pattern derives from both the presence of the dockyard and the high mobility levels among H.M. Services personnel. In addition, the Polytechnic, on the northern edge of the city centre, produces a transient student population in nearby inner city areas. It is also relevant that private rented housing is concentrated in the older parts of the city (see Fig. 31) and this tenure form is generally associated with high levels of turnover. By contrast, the wards with substantial local-authority housing estates, mainly in north-west Plymouth, stand out clearly on the map as zones with relatively few migrants. Turnover rates are customarily low in council housing: arranging transfers can be difficult and, unlike owner-occupiers, there are few financial incentives to trade up market.

Three
Employment & Unemployment

The Local Economy

The economy of Plymouth has traditionally depended on its naval dockyard and, to a lesser extent, on the city's role as a regional shopping and service centre. In the post-war period strenuous efforts have been made to widen and diversify the city's economic base but these have met with only partial success.

The dockyard extends over 330 acres along the eastern bank of the River Tamar and is the largest ship repair yard in western Europe. At the end of the war, it employed over 20,000 people but today despite the recent transfer of workers from Kent (following the closure of Chatham Dockyard), employment has fallen to little more than 12,000. Moreover, as part of its commitment to 'privatization', the Conservative Government is keen to introduce a form of commercial management to the dockyard and this is certain to lead to further substantial job losses. Many different estimates have been made as to the number of jobs at risk. The American-based company, Brown and Root, who now seem set to take over the yard have referred to the need to cut 4,200 jobs from the payroll, but at various times in the past figures of up to 7,000 have appeared in the local press. The precise position remains uncertain. Although the dockyard buys relatively little material or equipment from local firms, it injects through wages and salaries, about £2.5 million a week into the local economy. This spending in turn helps to sustain many other jobs in the city, especially in the retail and service sector. The threat of major cuts in the dockyard therefore casts a serious shadow over Plymouth's future.

In seeking to reduce the city's dependence on the dockyard, the local authority has concentrated its efforts on encouraging manufacturing industry to move to Plymouth or to establish branch plants here. Examples of firms attracted by this policy include Becton Dickinson (the medical suppliers) now at Belliver, Tecalemit (garage equipment manufacturers) now at Marsh Mills, Wrigley's (chewing gum manufacturers) at Estover and Plessey's who are building a micro-chip plant at Roborough. The new branch plants have 'internationalized' the local economy and the city now has 16 American companies, two from Germany and one from Japan.

Plymouth's diversification programme has been greatly helped by government grants and regional aid incentives which have played a key role in attracting new firms. Unfortunately, the recent downgrading of Plymouth to Intermediate Area status has, by reducing regional grants, made the task of diversification increasingly difficult at a time when new jobs are still more urgently needed. Moreover, the parched economic climate of the recession has dried up the stream of mobile industry which flowed more plentifully in earlier years.

The local authority is therefore pursuing a number of other economic policies including, for example, the encouragement of office development. With only 130,000 square feet (12,000m^2) of office floor space, Plymouth has one of the smallest office sectors of all provincial cities. Activities such as insurance, banking and financial services which have grown nationally are particularly poorly developed in Plymouth, the city's geographical remoteness having proved a serious handicap. In the public sector, Plymouth has lost out to Exeter where the office headquarters for the County Council and for the region's water, electricity and police services are established.

Other economic policies being pursued by the city council include the development of tourism, efforts to attract 'high-tech' industries and the encouragement of local entrepreneurship (a special small firms centre has been established in Stoke). The local authority also promotes the city by advertising its advantages: these include regional aid, a reliable workforce and a good industrial relations record, local training and higher education facilities, an attractive living and working environment, and improved communications including new air and ferry services. These undoubted benefits will not, however, be enough to avoid serious difficulties if the dockyard sheds more jobs. And no matter how energetic the local authority's policies, a major upturn in Plymouth's fortunes is unlikely without a secure future for the dockyard and increased growth in the national economy.

The Local Employment Structure

This table uses Census of Employment data to summarize the job structure of the Plymouth Travel to Work Area(TTWA). The TWWA has a population of about 300,000 and encompasses adjoining parts of southeast Cornwall, the South Hams and the lower Tamar Valley as well as the quarter of a million inhabitants in Plymouth itself. The location quotient column measures the area's degree of specialization in each particular employment category and has been calculated by dividing the percentage employed in each sector in the Plymouth TTWA by the corresponding percentage for the country as a whole. Thus, location quotients above 1.00 indicate that Plymouth has an above average involvement in a particular activity, and figures below 1.00 indicate a degree of under-representation.

By far the most significant item in the table is the location quotient of 20 for the category (X), shipbuilding (and repairing) and marine engineering. This industry, which in Plymouth is dominated by the naval dockyard, accounts for half the area's manufacturing jobs and 14 percent of total employment. Moreover, the table data underestimate the importance of defence related jobs because HM Armed Forces are excluded. If these were included, the location quotient for Public Administration and Defence (XXVII) would rise from 1.1 to about 9. Together, the dockyard and the armed forces account for approximately 25 per cent of all jobs in the Plymouth TTWA and a recent estimate by Paul Bishop of the Plymouth Polytechnic Business School suggests that allowing for multiplier effects they sustain one-third of the area's employment.

Also of note is the table's low location quotient for the business services category (XXIV) which nationally has been an important source of growth. The fact that less than a quarter of Plymouth's manufacturing location quotients exceed the parity figure of 1.00 confirms the narrowness of the area's employment base and points to a general lack of development in the local economy.

Employment in the Plymouth Travel to Work Area, 1981.

Order (sic 1968)		Employment 1981	Location Quotient
I, II	Total primary industries	2,272	.66
III	Food, drink & tobacco	2,744	.83
IV	Coal & petroleum products		
V	Chemicals & allied industries	475	.20
VI	Metal manufacturing		
VII	Mechanical engineering	4,142	.60
XIX	Other manufacturing		
VIII	Instrument engineering	1,076	1.67
IX	Electrical engineering	2,480	.72
X	Shipbuilding/ marine engineering	15,335	20.14
XI	Vehicles	140	.03
XII	Metal goods (other)	686	.29
XIII	Textiles		
XIV	Leather & fur goods	70	.06
XV	Clothing & footwear	1,595	1.15
XVI	Bricks, pottery & glass	595	0.50
XVII	Timber, furniture, etc.	702	0.60
XVIII	Paper, printing & publishing	1,554	0.58
	Total manufacturing industries	31,594	1.03
XX	Construction	6,193	1.08
XXI	Gas, electricity & water	1,981	1.13
XXII	Transport & communication	6,128	0.84
XXIII	Distributive trades	15,267	1.09
XXIV	Insurance, banking, finance & business services	4,881	0.74
XXV	Professional & scientific services	18,825	1.01
XXVI	Miscellaneous services	13,169	1.02
XXVII	Public admin. & defence	8,608	1.11
	Total service industries	68,859	1.00
	Unclassified by industry	81	-
	Total all industries	109,000	-

This table is reproduced by kind permission of Paul Bishop of the Plymouth Business School.

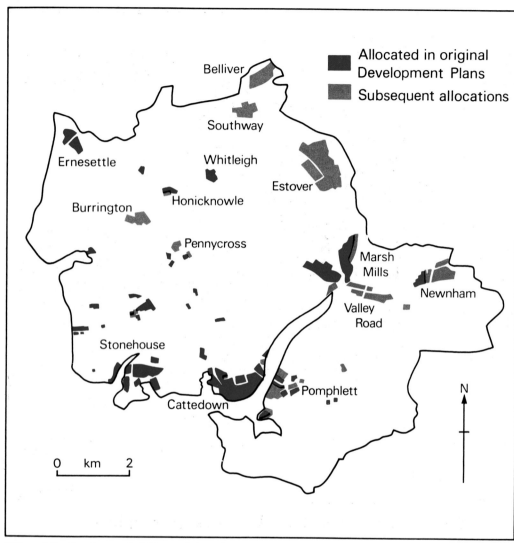

Allocated in original
Development Plans

Subsequent allocations

Belliver

Southway

Ernesettle

Whitleigh

Estover

Honicknowle

Burrington

Pennycross

Marsh
Mills

Newnham

Valley
Road

Stonehouse

Pomphlett

Cattedown

N

0   km   2

Fig. 19. Industrial Land in the City.

Fig. 19 (which excludes the dockyard and other Ministry of Defence establishments) summarises the spatial distribution of industrial land within the city. Before the war industry was concentrated around the waterfront areas in Stonehouse and Cattedown. The first post-war development plans made some additional land allocations, for example at Ernesettle, Whitleigh and Marsh Mills, but they seriously underestimated the amount of land which would be needed. In practice, more space was required both to accommodate incoming firms and to allow for the sharp fall in employment densities (due to technical changes and improving environmental standards). The new land has mainly taken the form of industrial estates in the northern and western suburbs as at Belliver, Estover and Newnham.

The dominance of the dockyard and Armed Forces, and the dearth of high-order business and management jobs have left their mark on the city's occupational and class structure. Social classes I and II account for only 23 per cent of Plymouth's population compared with a figure of 29 per cent for England and Wales. **Figs. 20** and **21** show where people of different socio-economic groups (SEGS) tend to live. The two 1981 census maps, which are broadly mirror images of each other, deal with households at opposite ends of the occupational spectrum (and omit groups such as skilled manual employees). The maps are based on heads of households' occupations and highlight Plymouth's predominant east-west social gradient with professionals in the east and less-skilled groups mainly in the west. There is also an inner city/suburban dimension with professional and semi-professional groups generally concentrated on the city's edge, though Compton, and to a lesser extent, Drake and Stoke are non-suburban areas with substantial professional populations. The highest proportions of semi-skilled and unskilled employees are mainly in areas with large council estates. Indeed, both maps are closely related to housing tenure patterns which are discussed in chapter four (see p. 46-48).

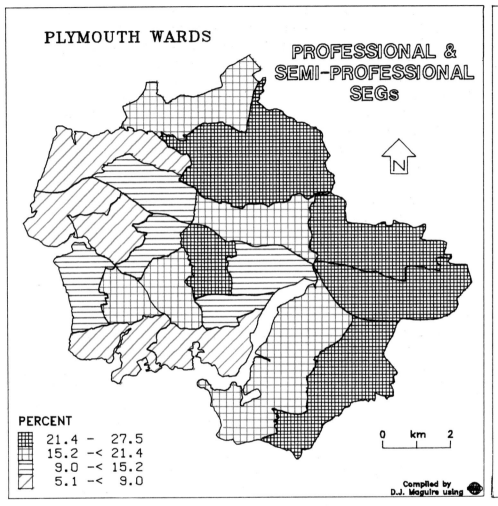

PLYMOUTH WARDS

PROFESSIONAL &
SEMI-PROFESSIONAL
SEGs

N

PERCENT

▦	21.4 – 27.5
	15.2 –< 21.4
	9.0 –< 15.2
	5.1 –< 9.0

0   km   2

Compiled by
D.J. Maguire using

Fig. 20. Professional and Semi-Professional Households.

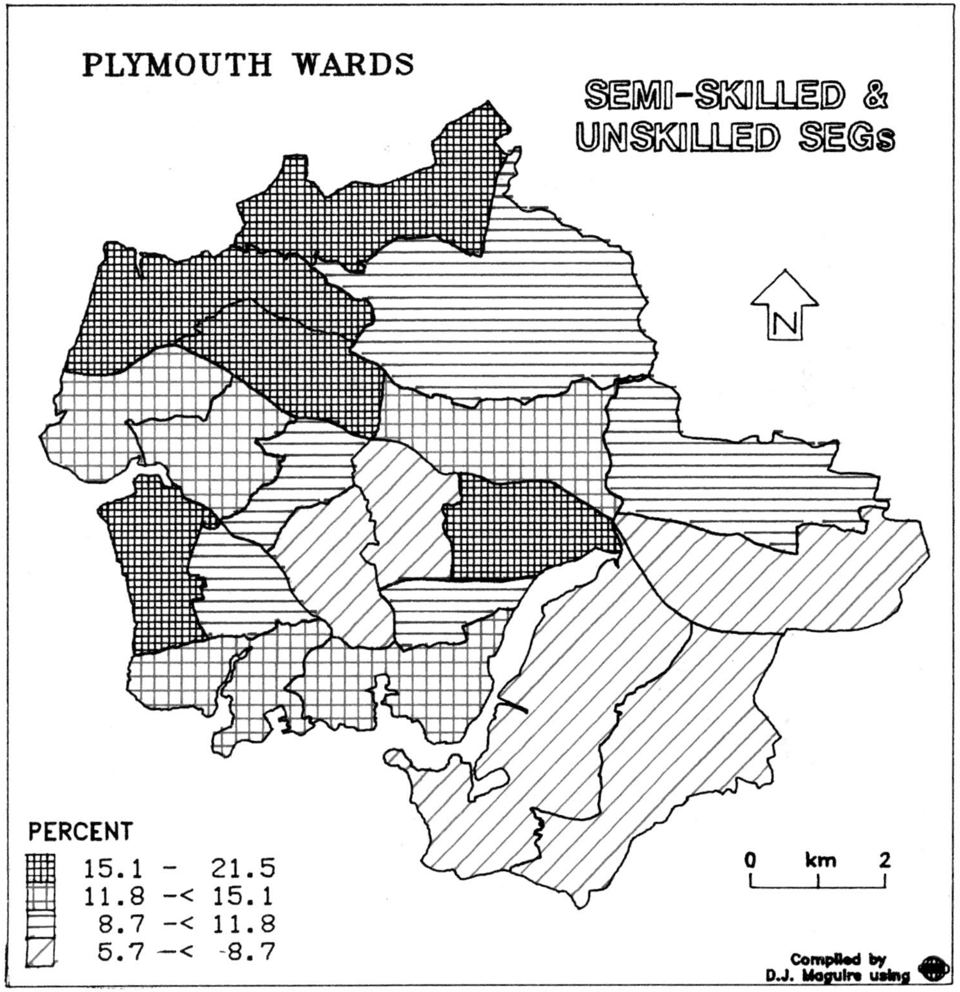

PLYMOUTH WARDS

SEMI-SKILLED &
UNSKILLED SEGs

N

PERCENT

▦	15.1 – 21.5
	11.8 –< 15.1
	8.7 –< 11.8
	5.7 –< 8.7

0   km   2

Compiled by
D.J. Maguire using

Fig. 21. Semi-Skilled and Unskilled Households.

35

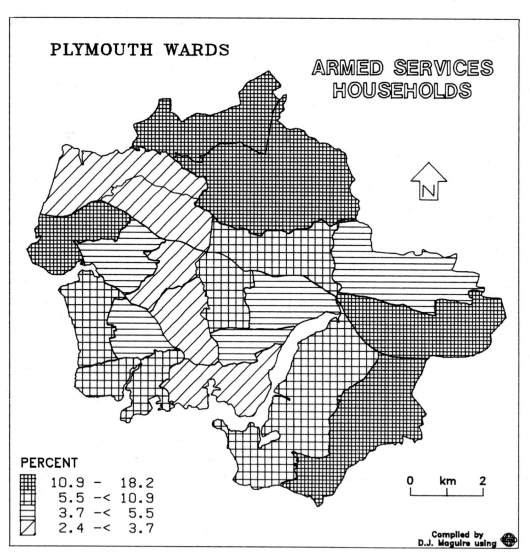

PLYMOUTH WARDS

ARMED SERVICES HOUSEHOLDS

N

PERCENT

10.9 – 18.2	
5.5 –< 10.9	
3.7 –< 5.5	
2.4 –< 3.7	

0   km   2

Compiled by
D.J. Maguire using

Fig. 22. Armed Services Households.

The Armed Services and in particular, the Royal Navy and Royal Marines, are an important and distinctive part of the local economy. Although little naval or military equipment is manufactured in Plymouth, the incomes of Armed Forces' personnel inject a substantial volume of spending power into the city. Moreover, given that many of the officers live in the surrounding small towns and villages, the economic benefits are not confined to the city alone.

The 1981 census (10 per cent sample data) indicates that there are in total about 5,300 Plymouth households (approximately seven per cent) which are headed by active or retired Armed Services personnel. The Ministry of Defence currently provides about 3,500 dwellings: these are spread across the city in a variety of locations but the largest estates are in St. Budeaux which has over 1,000 MOD dwellings. There is also substantial MOD provision in Crownhill (part of Estover Ward), Tamerton Foliot (in Southway Ward) and in Plympton and Plymstock. Not surprisingly these areas comprise the top category in **Fig. 22**. No new MOD housing is planned and this is because (in spite of the geographical mobility which characterizes life in the Armed Forces) there is a strong trend towards owner-occupation among Services personnel. The geography of Armed Forces households is therefore increasingly influenced by the spatial pattern of owner-occupied housing which in Plymouth tends to be especially dominant on the eastern side of the city (see Fig. 29).

Tourism

Tourism is another significant ingredient in the local economy, for although Plymouth is a working city rather than a resort (it has no beach), it is well situated to act as a base from which to explore the surrounding countryside, moors and coast. The city itself offers tourists a rich history and a range of modern facilities including shops, theatres, cinemas and restaurants. Plymouth's hotels, guest houses and self-catering accommodation together total over 7,000 bed spaces and another four star hotel, the Copthorne, is soon to open in the city centre.

The British Home Tourism Survey estimates that the city has an annual total of 2.6 million visitor nights which inject well over £20 million into the local economy. In addition, the city attracts large numbers of day visitors particularly on rainy summer days when the holidaymakers abandon the beaches and take refuge in the city's shops and cafes. Day visitors average about 9,000 on August weekdays and increase by 30 per cent in inclement weather.

Our MSC survey of summertime visitors to central Plymouth found that almost two-thirds were day visitors: less than three per cent of the people interviewed were staying in the city for more than a week. Average daily expenditure was estimated at £17 per head with most being spent in the city's shops and restaurants. Nonetheless, only 14 per cent of visitors had come to Plymouth primarily for shopping purposes. In practice, by far the most common visitor activity was "general sight-seeing" (61 per cent). It was interesting that although most visitors were aware of The Hoe and of Plymouth's historical associations, few had come with a clear idea of particular places to see. This no doubt reflects the absence in Plymouth of major visitor centre-pieces: there is no equivalent to York Minster or the Mary Rose. Equally, there are no theme parks or large-scale leisure centres and this dearth of attractions for young people may in part account for the fact that 55 per cent of visitors in our survey were aged 45 and over.

Within Plymouth there is clearly scope for further tourism development and the local authority has begun an ambitious programme designed to remedy the significant deficiencies in what the city currently offers. It is recognised, of course, that Plymouth cannot compete in the "sun, sea and sand" holiday market, but there are many opportunities for capitalizing on the city's history and for exploiting current trends in tourism such as the growth of short and off-peak breaks, activity and special interest holidays and the development of large-scale visitor attractions. In addition to the need for improved facilities, Plymouth is keen to strengthen further its marketing and information services. (In the survey of tourists in Plymouth only one in six visitors had seen any promotional literature and less than one in twelve had been to the Tourism Information Centres). In the past because of the proximity of seaside resorts Plymouth has, almost inadvertently benefited from tourism at second hand: in future the city intends to be a holiday centre in its own right.

As part of this new approach a marina has been built at Queen Anne's Battery to provide an attractive setting for Plymouth to host international sailing events. A marine walk is planned around Sutton Pool, reminiscent perhaps of San Francisco's famous fisherman's wharf. At Millbay a £16 million leisure complex is to be built and, in the city centre, an ambitious programme of pedestrianisation and other improvements will provide a more attractive environment for tourists and locals alike. And on The Hoe there is to be a visitor centre which will interpret Plymouth's history and illustrate famous scenes from the past, including the defeat of the Spanish Armada. In July 1988 the city intends to celebrate in style the 400th anniversary of Drake's victory and a variety of special events are being planned to attract large numbers of visitors.

By all these and other means it is hoped that tourism will play a significant part in diversifying Plymouth's employment base. Some of the new jobs will, of course, be seasonal and relatively few will be highly paid. Nonetheless, tourism looks certain in future to play a larger role in the local economy and the city's Marketing Bureau is working hard to put Plymouth firmly on the tourist's map.

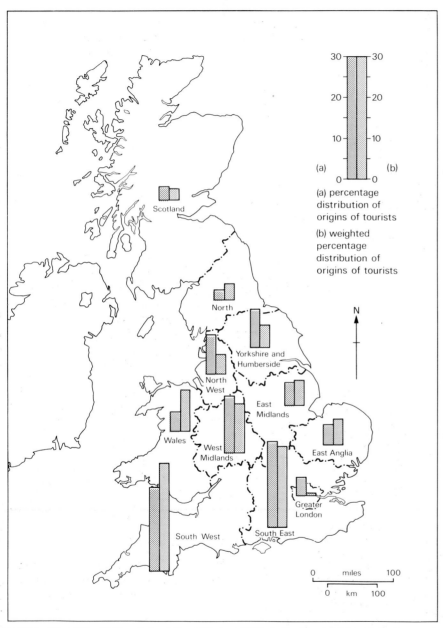

(a) percentage distribution of origins of tourists

(b) weighted percentage distribution of origins of tourists

Fig. 23. Plymouth's Tourists: The Source Areas.

Fig. 23 uses MSC survey data to identify the home areas of visitors to Plymouth. In broad terms it reveals a pattern of "distance decay" with the South West, South East and West Midlands being the dominant regions whether measured by simple percentages or by a weighted index taking into account each area's resident population size. The map does not, of course, include the survey's nine per cent of overseas visitors, most of whom were from France (utilising the Roscoff-Plymouth ferry service) or from the USA (attracted perhaps by Plymouth's history and its link with the Pilgrim Fathers).

Fig. 24 itemises the places most frequently visited by the people interviewed in the MSC survey. Within central Plymouth the high figures for The Hoe and the Barbican augur well for the new Hoe visitor centre and for the Sutton Pool marine walk. Equally, however, the overwhelming dominance of the traditional tourist venues points up the need for some alternative kinds of visitor experience such as theme parks. The proposed Millbay leisure complex should help to meet this requirement. Outside central Plymouth, as Fig. 24 indicates, the city is reasonably well served by a variety of attractions in the surrounding areas (including for example, Dartmoor, Buckland Abbey, the Shire Horse Centre and many others). With a strengthening of the city's own facilities, Plymouth has the opportunity to offer tourists who stay here a powerful package of both city-based and peripheral attractions.

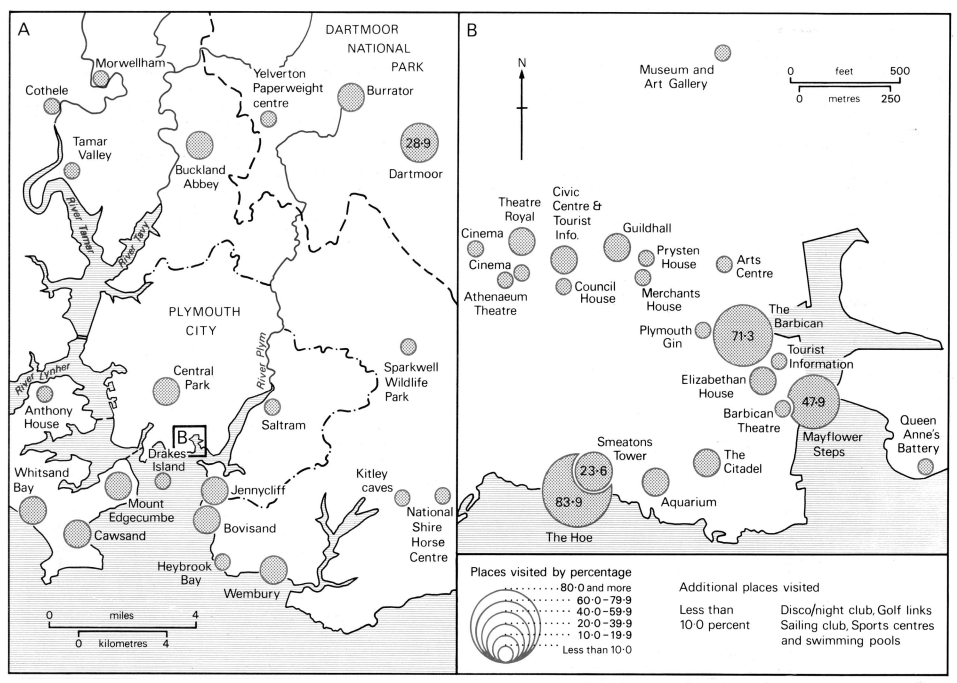

Fig. 24. Tourist Attractions in the Plymouth Region.

Unemployment in the City

As the national rate of unemployment has risen in recent years so the dole queues have lengthened in Plymouth. The August 1986 figures for the Plymouth TTWA showed that 11,772, or 16.6 per cent, of the male population was unemployed and 6,988, or 13.2 per cent, of the female population. If, as some fear, a further 7,000 jobs are to be lost in the dockyard, it is estimated that an additional 3,000 jobs would be lost in the service and retail sectors. On this basis the total unemployment rate could therefore reach between 23 and 24 per cent.

Future unemployment levels are obviously uncertain but irrespective of any employment changes in the dockyard or other local industries, there are two considerations which will make reducing the city's dole queues especially difficult. The first is that Plymouth has a relatively small proportion of its population in the pre-retirement age groups and yet an average proportion of school children. The demand from school leavers will therefore inevitably outstrip the supply of jobs released on retirement. The second negative factor is that Plymouth's traditionally low "female activity rate" is expected to rise in future: this increase in the proportion of women wanting employment will intensify the need for new jobs.

The unemployment maps, **Figs. 25** and **26,** are for July 1985 and were based on a data system whose geographical units and place names were unfortunately not directly comparable with those of the census. The data were produced by the Department of Employment's Joint Unemployment and Vacancies Operating System (JUVOS) and were made available by the Economic and Social Research Council's Data Archive at Essex University. The highest proportion unemployed, nearly 28 per cent, in the Stonehouse and Devonport areas, is about four times the lowest figure of 7 per cent for Plympton. The areas with the worst unemployment rate tend to be those with a high proportion of people whose usual occupation is semi-skilled or unskilled, and those with a high proportion of young adults. These groups, who are especially vulnerable to unemployment, tend to be concentrated in the western half of the city and especially in the inner urban area. It is noticeable that the Ham area, which includes part of the North Prospect council estate, forms a detached outlier of particularly acute unemployment levels. This may not be unrelated to the fact that North Prospect has on a number of occasions been the scene of civil disturbances and conflict between young people and the police. Given that many dockyard employees live near their work on this western side of the city, further dockyard redundacies would exacerbate unemployment in the areas already hardest hit, thereby further raising social tensions and intensifying the inequalities between east and west Plymouth.

In assessing spatial variations in the severity of unemployment, account should be taken not only of the percentage rate but also of the absolute numbers. It is also important to identify the long-term unemployed (here defined as a year or more) since many in this group obviously face especially severe economic and personal difficulties: moreover, the longer the period of unemployment the less the chance of getting back successfully into the labour market.

Fig. 26 again illustrates both the large scale of unemployment in the older inner areas of Stonehouse, Devonport, North Hill and Cattedown, and the most privileged position of Plympton and Plymstock. In these two eastern suburbs not only are the total numbers at their lowest but so is the proportion of unemployed who are long-term (23 and 26 per cent respectively compared with 37 per cent for Plymouth as a whole). At the other end of the spectrum, the Stonehouse and Devonport area has the largest number unemployed, over 2,500, of whom 46 per cent are long-term, a proportion exceeded only in Ham, which once again therefore emerges as an area of special concern.

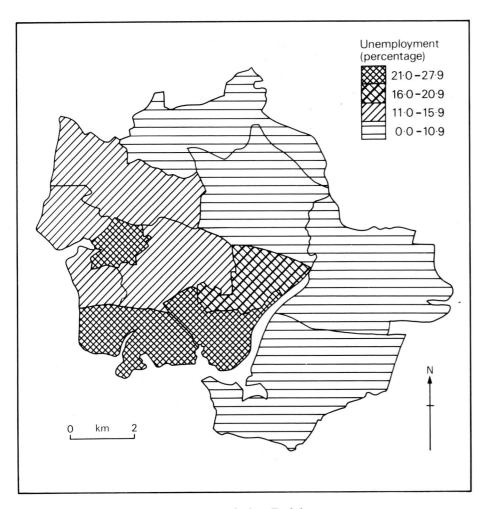

Fig. 25. The Distribution of the Jobless: The % Unemployed.

Unemployment (percentage)
21·0 – 27·9
16·0 – 20·9
11·0 – 15·9
0·0 – 10·9

0   km   2

N

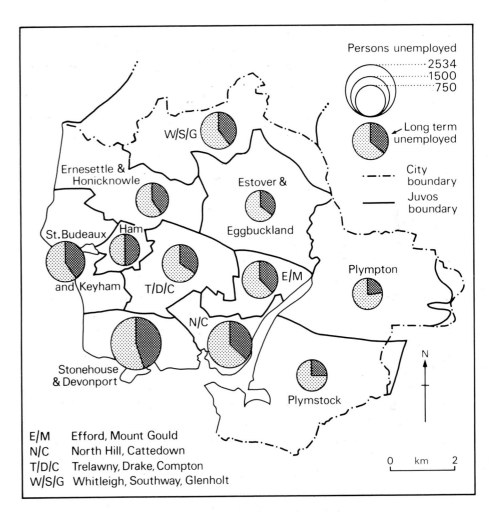

Fig. 26. The Numbers Unemployed: Long-term & Short-term.

Persons unemployed
2534
1500
750

Long term unemployed

City boundary

Juvos boundary

W/S/G
Ernesettle & Honicknowle
Estover & Eggbuckland
St. Budeaux and Keyham
Ham
E/M
Plympton
T/D/C
N/C
Stonehouse & Devonport
Plymstock

E/M   Efford, Mount Gould
N/C   North Hill, Cattedown
T/D/C Trelawny, Drake, Compton
W/S/G Whitleigh, Southway, Glenholt

N

0   km   2

Four
**The Housing
Stock**

The Housing Stock

As with all cities, Plymouth's present-day housing stock is in large measure the product of building decisions made in the past. This housing legacy provides a tangible, if incomplete, record of the city's historical development, particularly over the last 150 years.

About a quarter of the city's housing was built before 1914. Most of these older dwellings are found in the inner urban areas and in small outliers which mark the cores of previously separate settlements, such as Tamerton Foliot and Plympton, which have been engulfed by Plymouth's outward expansion. Indeed, until the late nineteenth century even Devonport and Stonehouse were geographically detached from Plymouth, the gradual coalescence of the three towns resulting in 1914 in their administrative unification. At this stage, the city was characterised mainly by large areas of working-class, bye-law housing whose densities often reached 20 dwellings per acre. By contrast, the Mannamead area with its large villas had already acquired a reputation as the city's premier, high-status residential area. By the time of World War One, Peverell, about two miles from the city centre, marked Plymouth's northern frontier.

In the years immediately after the war the local authority began to play an increasingly significant role in housing provision. With sailors and soldiers returning home, the peace-time campaign was for "homes fit for heroes to live in". Work began on the North Prospect estate in 1919 and by 1939 Plymouth had nearly 5,000 council dwellings. Most were on the city's edge and built, with gardens, at the relatively low density of about ten to the acre. Some, however, were built as flats mainly on slum clearance sites in the inner city. For all its importance, local-authority housing was, however, heavily outnumbered in the inter-war years by private sector developments as at Compton, Pennycross, Peverell and St. Budeaux. In addition, Plympton and Plymstock were expanded from quiet villages to substantial suburbs. Overall about one-fifth of the city's present housing stock is of inter-war origin.

Since 1945 Plymouth's built-up area has more than doubled. This expansion has been primarily due to reductions in overcrowding and to the planned dispersal of population from the congested inner city. The local-authority estates at Efford, Ernesettle, Ham, Honicknowle and Whitleigh were built on the neighbourhood unit principles discussed earlier (see pages 16 - 19). Later council estates such as those at Southway, Leigham and Estover, incorporated a number of design changes including more off-street parking and garage spaces and a return to higher residential densities. In recent years house building in the public sector has been on a much reduced scale but there has been considerable activity in the private sector especially in the north and east of the city in areas such as Roborough, Estover, Plympton and Plymstock. **Figs.** 27 and 28 on housing type utilise data obtained in a major MSC household survey (see Technical Appendix for details). Although based on only sample evidence from selected areas, a number of general patterns are clearly evident. The terrace is the city's most common building form (43 per cent) and it is particulary dominant in an east-west band stretching from Keyham and Devonport across to Peverell, Lipson and Laira (readers unfamiliar with Plymouth are reminded of the place name map on page 6). The Mutley area, to the north of the Polytechnic, is the zone with the highest proportion of converted flats, many terraced houses having been sub-divided to meet student demand. Purpose-built flats (a relatively rare phenomenon in Plymouth) predominate in the Mount Wise area where most of Plymouth's high-rise blocks are concentrated. By contrast, the purpose-built flats in central Plymouth rarely exceed four storeys. Semi-detached housing is spread across much of northern and eastern Plymouth but is especially characteristic of Plympton and Plymstock. It is very noticeable that detached housing is virtually absent on the western side of the city. Instead, it too is commonplace in Plympton and Plymstock and in a line which begins with the Victorian villas of Compton and Mannamead and runs north through Crownhill and out to Glenholt.

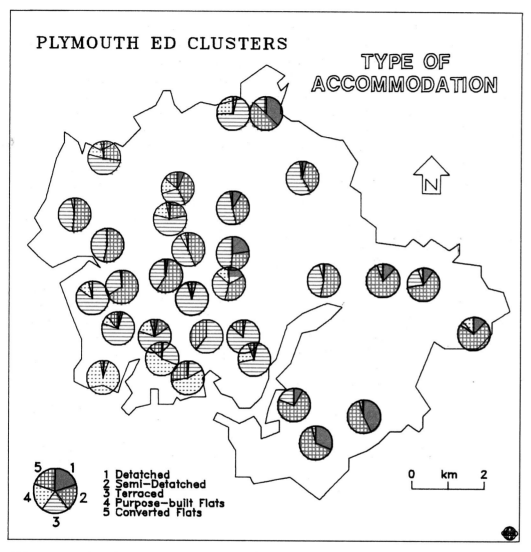

Fig. 27. The Spatial Pattern of Dwelling Types.

PLYMOUTH ED CLUSTERS

TYPE OF ACCOMMODATION

1 Detatched
2 Semi-Detatched
3 Terraced
4 Purpose-built Flats
5 Converted Flats

0   km   2

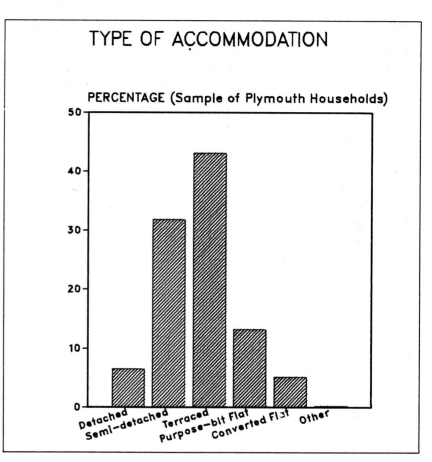

TYPE OF ACCOMMODATION

PERCENTAGE (Sample of Plymouth Households)

Fig. 28. Type of Accommodation.

Housing Tenure

The form of ownership is one of the most important housing characteristics and is of considerable significance economically, socially and politically: house purchase is for many families the biggest financial decision they make, the form of tenure is often used as a measure of social status, and issues such as council house sales and mortgage tax relief are among the most contentious and sensitive on the national political agenda.

The table below shows clearly that the overall tenure pattern in Plymouth is not dissimilar to the national average. Locally and nationally owner occupation is now the majority tenure, council housing accommodates rather less than one-third of all households and the private-rented sector accounts for most of the rest. Owner-occupation levels have been rising across the country and the Plymouth figure increased from 44.7 per cent to 55.2 per cent between the 1971 and 1981 censuses. Plymouth's council house sector, although slightly smaller than the national norm, is large by Devon standards. Indeed, Plymouth has a higher proportion of council dwellings than any other Devon District. This reflects the usual pattern of urban areas having a higher percentage of council housing than rural areas. Plymouth currently has over 22,000 council houses, having sold to tenants nearly 7,000, half of these since the "Right to Buy" legislation. In the case of privately-rented housing both Plymouth and Devon have shared in the nationwide contraction of this sector, although in Plymouth the presence of HM Forces and large numbers of students has helped to keep the figure a little above the Great Britain average.

The aggregate Plymouth data on housing tenure conceal, of course, some very striking contrasts between different parts of the city. For example, owner-occupation levels range from 90.5 per cent of all households in Plympton St. Mary to only 15.7 per cent in St. Peter. The geography of owner-occupation as shown in **Fig. 29,** picks out Plympton, Plymstock and the Compton ward (which includes Mannamead) as the areas with the highest figures. It should be noted, however, that some particularly high-status, owner-occupation areas (such as Glenholt and nearby Derriford) fail to stand out because of their inclusion within wards of a more varied tenure structure. Medium levels of owner-occupation are characteristic of an east-west band from Keyham to Mount Gould, a zone which includes much of the pre-1914 stock of terraced housing. The lowest owner-occupation figures are in the north-west and in the inner city. The highly uneven distribution portrayed in Fig. 29 reflects, of course, the uneven distribution of purchasing power and of access to mortgage facilities.

Fig. 30 shows that the geography of council housing is almost a reverse image of that for owner-occupation. The percentage of households in local-authority dwellings varies from 75.2 in Budshead to 1.09 in Compton. This near 70 fold difference indicates a degree of spatial unevenness which is even more pronounced than that for owner-occupation. There are areas of the city where council housing is virtually absent. The lowest council figures are in those older parts of the city where the housing stock has been of sufficiently good quality to avoid local-authority urban redevelopment programmes. In these areas there has been little space, opportunity or need for local-authority provision. By contrast, council housing is the dominant tenure in the neighbourhood units in the north-west suburbs and also in the inner city ward of St. Peter where first bomb damage and then slum clearance led to extensive local-authority provision.

Housing Tenure, 1981

	Plymouth	Devon	Great Britain
Owner occupied	55.2%	63.9%	55.7%
Council	27.1%	20.1%	31.2%
Private rented	14.7%	11.4%	8.6%
Other	3.0%	4.6%	4.2%

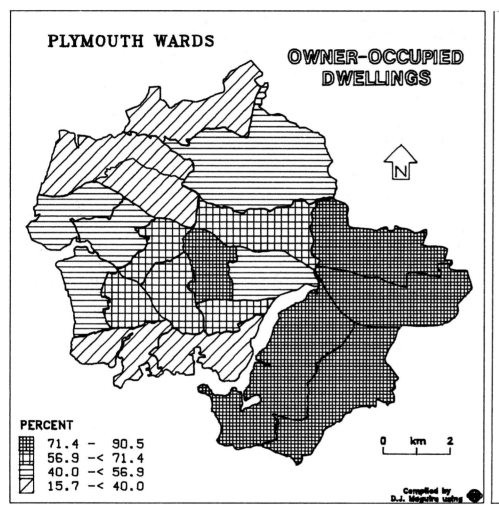

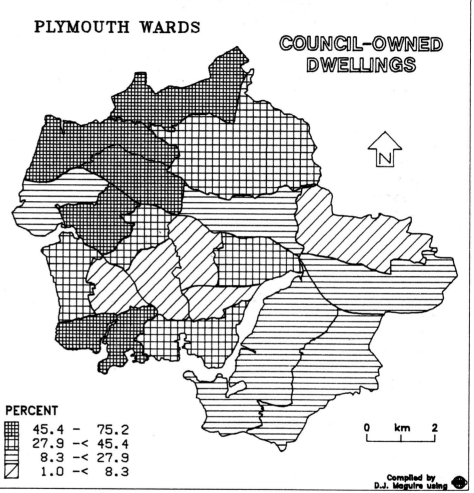

Fig. 29. Owner-Occupied Dwellings.

Fig. 30. Council-Owned Dwellings.

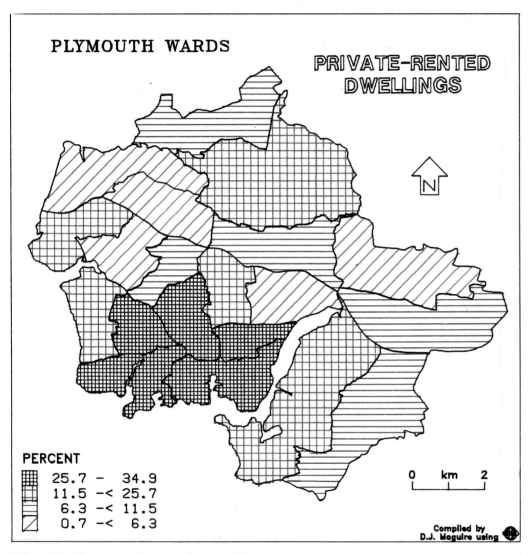

PLYMOUTH WARDS

PRIVATE-RENTED DWELLINGS

N

PERCENT

25.7 -   34.9
11.5 -< 25.7
 6.3 -< 11.5
 0.7 -<   6.3

0   km   2

Compiled by
D.J. Maguire using

Fig. 31. Private-Rented Dwellings.

In Plymouth, as in other cities, the proportion of private-rented housing has been in long-term decline principally because of government legislation on rent controls and security of tenure for tenants. Renting out housing has often not therefore produced monetary returns comparable with other kinds of financial investment. Nonetheless, **Fig. 31** shows that private-rented housing is still of considerable significance in Plymouth's inner city wards: it reaches a maximum figure of nearly 35 per cent of all households in Drake which includes most of Mutley an area dominated by large pre-1914 houses sub-divided into flats and bed-sitters.

The growth of the Polytechnic, on the northern edge of the city centre, has played a key role in sustaining the private-rented sector. The Polytechnic now has over 4,900 full-time and sandwich students drawn from many parts of the country but is able to offer only 635 places in its own student residences (by the standards of other Polytechnics and Universities, this is an unusually low proportion). As a result, there is a large demand for both lodgings and flats especially in inner urban areas close to the Polytechnic. By comparison, in many suburban wards dwellings have been built for owner occupation or council housing. The lowest private-rented figure is 0.7 per cent for Budshead.

For a more detailed view of the geography of tenure, it is helpful to change the focus down to the scale of enumeration districts. **Fig. 32** serves to illustrate the range of homogeneity and heterogeneity which can be found at this more local level. Some parts of the city possess a fairly uniform housing stock: in other areas the position varies almost street by street.

The map of the southern part of Keyham (including the Park Avenue area) reveals a consistently low percentage of owner occupation. This is an area where comprehensive redevelopment led to substantial tracts of local authority housing. The eastern portion of Plympton Erle (in the area of Yeoman's Way) also has a homogeneous housing structure, in this case with consistently high levels of owner occupation. By contrast the western part of Honicknowle (straddling the Crownhill Road and the Eastbury Avenue and Ringmore Way areas) shows a remarkably varied pattern with very high and very low levels of owner occupation next to each other. Here a mixture of public and private housing development has produced a much more heterogeneous pattern whose presence is concealed by ward-level averages.

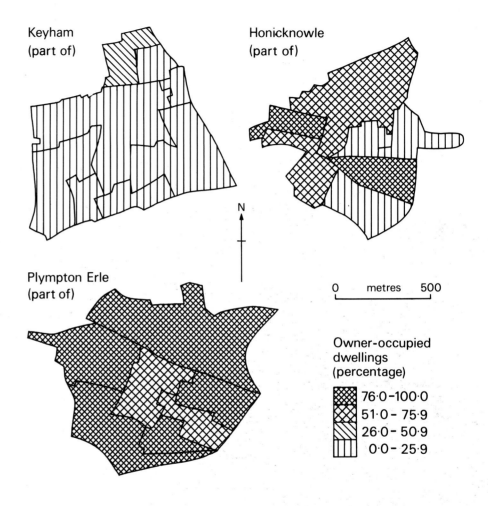

Fig. 32. Local Variations in the Level of Owner-Occupation.

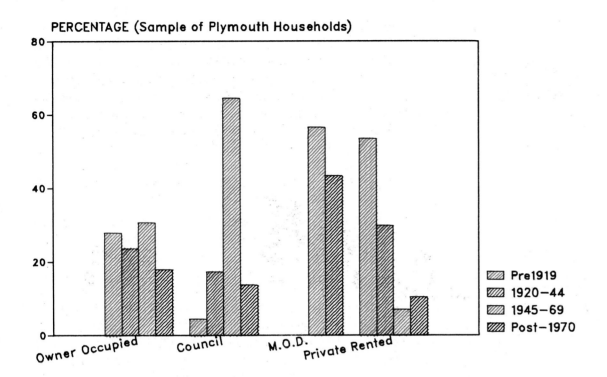

PERCENTAGE (Sample of Plymouth Households)

Legend:
- Pre1919
- 1920-44
- 1945-69
- Post-1970

Categories: Owner Occupied, Council, M.O.D., Private Rented

Fig. 33. Age of Dwellings by Tenure.

Although based on the evidence of a sample survey, **Fig. 33** provides a useful guide to the age profile of the different types of tenure. It identifies the contribution made by each period to the dwelling stock of each tenure category (though remember that these tenure categories are of different sizes). In the case of owner-occupied dwellings Fig. 33 shows that all the periods have made a broadly similar contribution to the present-day stock. By contrast, about two-thirds of the city's council dwellings date from the 1945 - 1969 period which includes the era of neighbourhood unit building. The smaller number of pre-First World War council dwellings (as for example in the Barbican and at Prince Rock) were provided by the Housing of the Working Classes Committee: this was established in 1893 to build artisans dwellings and was the forerunner of today's Housing Committee. The Ministry of Defence dwellings are all post-1945. By contrast, over half the private-rented accommodation pre-dates World War One.

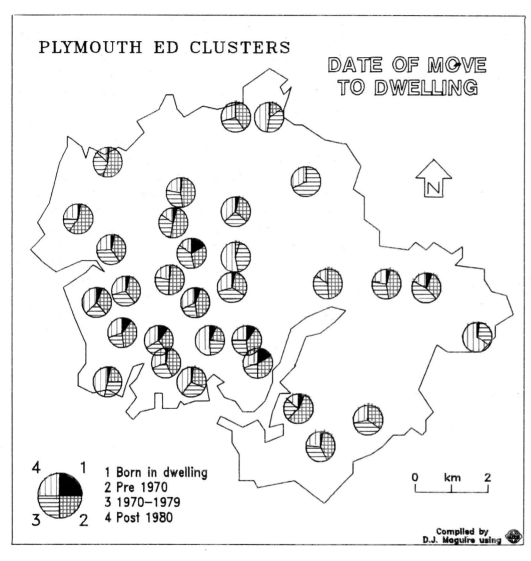

PLYMOUTH ED CLUSTERS

DATE OF MOVE TO DWELLING

N

4   1   1 Born in dwelling
             2 Pre 1970
3   2   3 1970–1979
             4 Post 1980

0   km   2

Compiled by
D.J. Maguire using

Fig. 34. Date of Move to Dwelling.

In addition to information on the age of the housing stock, the sample survey provided information on the date at which heads of households had moved into their present dwellings. The results confirm the generally high levels of mobility referred to in chapter two, with most household heads having moved into their existing accommodation since 1970. Indeed, in only six of the 31 areas sampled did the majority of resident households pre-date 1970. This illustrates very clearly the difficulty in today's society of building up stable communities with high proportions of long established residents.

Fig. 34 shows that the spatial pattern of length of residence is complex with few unambiguous trends and many local variations. As one would expect, however, residence times are at their lowest in the newest housing areas such as Estover and eastern Plympton. Some inner city areas also have a high proportion of recent arrivals and in the Mutley area, at the centre of Plymouth's "bedsit land", three-quarters of the population are post-1980 residents. It is noticeable that in most parts of Plymouth there are few, if any, household heads living at the address at which they were born, the only exception being the zone of old terraced housing stretching from Devonport across to Lipson and Laira. But even here the figures average only about ten per cent. Plymouth residents are clearly people on the move.

Five
Housing Conditions

Housing Conditions

Housing conditions are of immense importance in shaping the quality of people's everyday lives. Poor housing can produce not only physical discomfort but also social and domestic tensions and, in extreme cases, psychological stress and health problems. It is important therefore to have reliable information on housing quality in order to identify those areas where improvements are most needed. The Population Census provides a number of helpful indicators of housing conditions (some of which are mapped in this chapter) but it is an insufficient guide in two significant respects. First, its range of housing indicators is limited and many important features are omitted: for example, there is no information on problems such as damp or condensation, or on heating arrangements and insulation levels. A second weakness is that the kinds of physical indicators used in the census can never measure the actual experience of living in poor surroundings or gauge people's perception and evaluation of their housing conditions. The MSC household survey was therefore undertaken to remedy these deficiencies and so this chapter is able to draw on both census and special survey data in order to provide a fuller picture of housing conditions in Plymouth.

Historically Plymouth's housing has had an unenviable reputation and the city's rapid growth in the nineteenth century led to particularly grim conditions. As late as 1931 the local Medical Officer of Health reported that there were on average 1.7 families for each house, and overcrowding was as severe as in any of Britain's major industrial cities. Today by contrast Plymouth is relatively well housed and on most Census indicators the city is close to or better than the national average.

Certainly, there are no large areas of unfit housing left in the city. This improvement owes much to the success of post-war town planning policies. A major slum clearance programme eliminated much of the worst legacy of Victorian housing and between 1952 and 1962 the city demolished 1,200 unfit dwellings and a further 300 that were deemed to be in very poor condition. In recent years many older houses have been renovated and their amenities upgraded with the help of home improvement grants. In addition, the city has designated eight General Improvement Areas in which special efforts are made to enhance the local environment and landscape. Pre-war council estates have been modernised and the local authority has begun to upgrade its post-war stock. Above all, the major programmes of new house building by local authority, the Ministry of Defence and private developers have played a key role in improving housing conditions.

Nonetheless, the city is not without its housing problems and for the unfortunate minority in highly unsatisfactory dwellings there is little comfort in the knowledge that conditions are often even worse in other cities. Moreover, within Plymouth housing standards are generally lowest in those areas which experience other problems too such as unemployment, poverty and unattractive environments.

Fig. 35 shows one of the most commonly used indicators of housing stress, namely the proportion of households not in self-contained accommodation. The overall average is 5.2. per cent (4798 households) and this is one problem which is more acute in Plymouth than in most other parts of the country. This derives from the city's above average proportion of private-rented flats and hence non-self-contained dwellings are most common in Drake Ward at the centre of the city's main 'bed-sit' area.

Fig. 36 shows another key indicator of housing stress, namely the proportion of households lacking a bath or an inside toilet. The overall figure is 1.8 per cent which represents some 1,754 households. Although large areas of the city are virtually free from the problem it is noticeably more prevalent in the inner city and in Sutton Ward it affects 5.9 per cent of all households. Although about half the dwellings concerned are in the private rented sector, some two-fifths are owner-occupied and presumably belong to households (many of them elderly) lacking either the resources or the inclination to upgrade their properties.

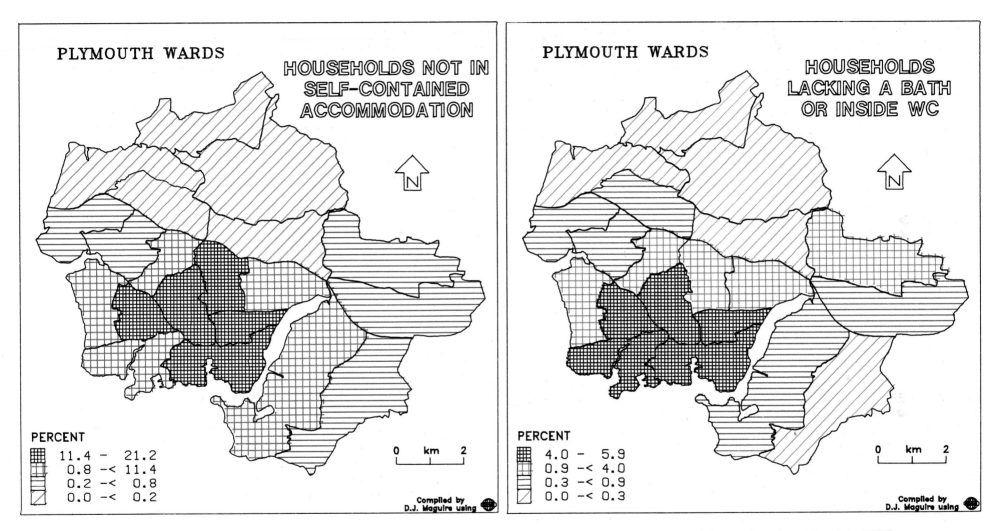

Fig. 35. Households Not in Self-Contained Accommodation. Fig. 36. Households Lacking a Bath or Inside WC.

Households living at densities of more than 1.5 persons per room (see **Fig. 37**) are conventionally regarded as suffering from serious overcrowding. The city rate is a mere 0.6 per cent (534 households), a very low figure which indicates the success of post-war policies in reducing overcrowding. Again, about half the households affected are in the private-rented sector but another third are in council dwellings and presumably include families awaiting a transfer to more spacious council accommodation. Most of Plymouth's overcrowded households are in the inner city with, by contrast, the lowest figures being found in Plympton, Plymstock and Estover.

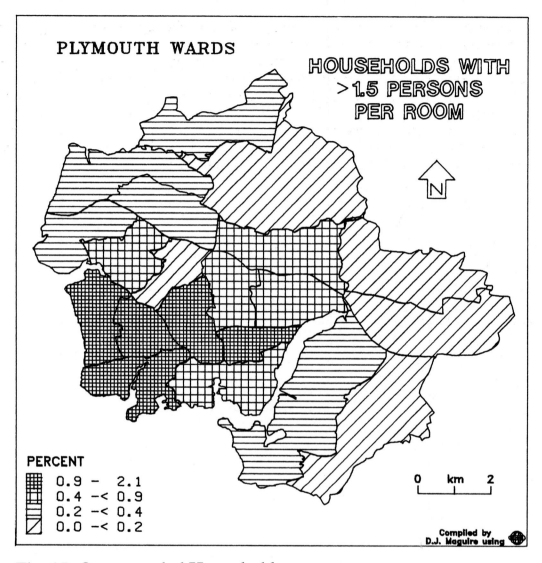

PLYMOUTH WARDS

HOUSEHOLDS WITH
>1.5 PERSONS
PER ROOM

N

PERCENT
0.9 - 2.1
0.4 -< 0.9
0.2 -< 0.4
0.0 -< 0.2

0   km   2

Compiled by
D.J. Maguire using

Fig. 37. Overcrowded Households.

Damp, Heating and Insulation

To live in a house which is free from damp and has a satisfactory system of heating and insulation must rank amongst the most important requirements for a decent standard of living in contemporary Britain. The Plymouth household survey sought therefore to find out how serious and widespread are the problems of damp and condensation in the city's housing stock: in addition, information was obtained on heating systems and the extent of home insulation. The aggregate figures and the spatial variations which emerged (see Figs 38-43) provide further useful insights into the quality of Plymouth's housing.

As a result of the city's maritime location and its relatively high rainfall and humidity levels, Plymouth's housing stock is especially prone to damp. The problem takes two forms: structural damp makes its way through the floor, walls or roof, whereas condensation occurs when air inside the home cools to its dew point. Structural damp, whether it is rising, penetrating or percolating, results from weaknesses in the building's fabric or the absence of a proper damp course. Condensation, however, can result from the occupants' lifestyles and the heating and washing arrangements, though it can be made worse by certain building materials and by inadequate ventilation. In the specially commissioned MSC survey 23 per cent of households reported structural damp and in a third of these cases (one in twelve of all interviewed households) the problem was considered serious. Nearly 34 per cent of households were troubled by condensation and again one third of these (10 per cent of the total sample) regarded the problem as serious. It is possible, of course, that some households mistook damp for condensation and certainly more detailed enquiries would be necessary to quantify the precise extent of these problems. Nonetheless, the results do provide a pointer to the scale of two problems which are likely not only to impair health and comfort, but also to result in building deterioration and costly repairs if not dealt with in time. There are, of course, home improvement grants towards the cost of work to remedy serious damp, condensation and other housing defects but it is clear that the grants system has so far failed to provide a complete solution.

It is interesting that the problems of damp and condensation persist in spite of rising standards of home heating. Indeed, better insulation may have made things worse by reducing ventilation. The survey showed that the proportion of Plymouth households who have some form of central heating has risen to 57 per cent with figures exceeding 80 per cent in parts of Plympton and Plymstock. Insulation standards have risen too. Building regulations have become increasingly strict about insulation levels in new dwellings and many owners of existing properties have also invested in some form of insulation. Our survey found that roof insulation was present in 84 per cent of dwellings for which this kind of measure was appropriate. This high figure reflects the relatively low costs involved and the availability of special government grants. For double glazing, which is much more expensive and attracts no grants, the figure was only 28 per cent and for wall insulation only 7 per cent.

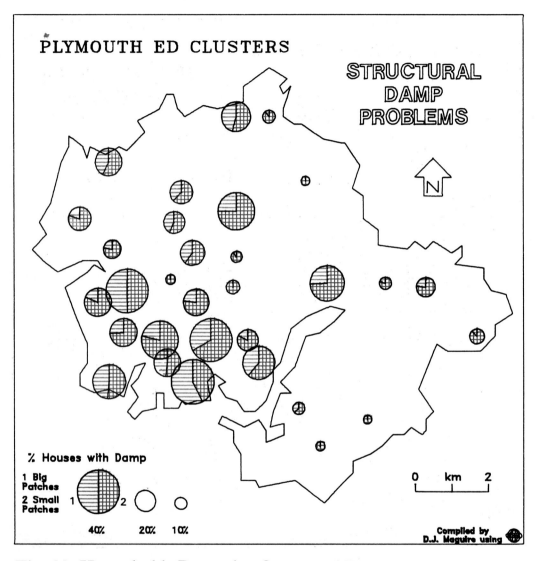

Fig. 38. Households Reporting Structural Damp.

Structural damp (**Fig. 38**) is heavily concentrated on the western side of Plymouth and especially in the inner city areas near the coast. The explanation, however, lies not in the prevailing westerly winds or in local rainfall variations but in the age and tenure of buildings. Over one-third of pre-1919 dwellings were reported as suffering from damp as compared with only 14 per cent of the post-1970 stock. Owner-occupiers, who predominate in eastern Plymouth, reported the lowest figure (15 per cent), whereas for private and council tenants the figures were 46 per cent and 33 per cent respectively reporting at least some degree of damp.

The 'geography of condensation' (**Fig. 39**) is considerably different from that of damp. Although Plympton, Plymstock and Estover are once again little affected, it is noticeable that condensation shows no concentration in the inner city. Here the older stock of dwellings, with their open fireplaces, sash windows and high ceilings, benefits from good ventilation. By contrast, some of the northern suburbs are much worse affected. At Southway, for example, many of the 1960s council dwellings were the product of a 'system building' form of construction which has not worked well. The warm air heating systems are costly to run and are therefore often not used: this leads to condensation. Tenants in such areas may feel they have a choice between condensation and mould if the heating is turned off, and bills they cannot afford if it is turned on. The local authority is giving attention to this problem but overall can consider itself fortunate that much of the council housing stock was built in the early post-war years by more traditional construction methods.

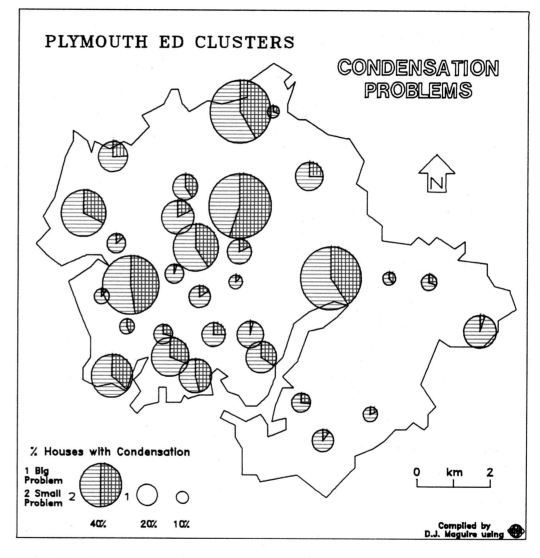

Fig. 39. Households Reporting Condensation.

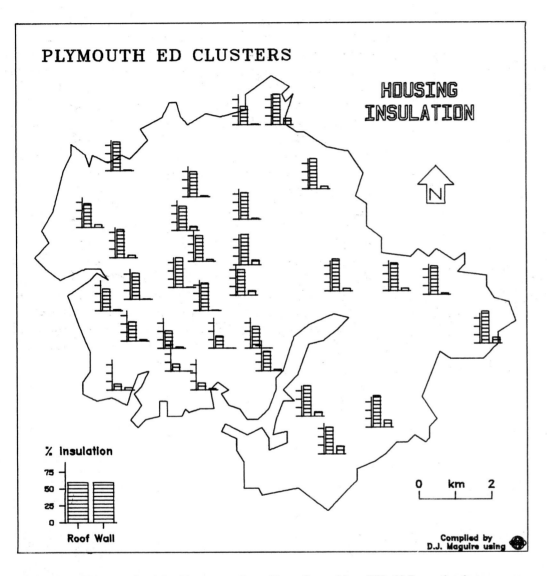

PLYMOUTH ED CLUSTERS

HOUSING INSULATION

N

% Insulation

75
50
25
0

Roof Wall

0   km   2

Compiled by
D.J. Maguire using

As **Fig. 40** shows, roof insulation is more common than wall insulation throughout the city. Roof insulation is cheaper and attracts government grants: moreover, special measures to insulate the walls are in many cases unnecessary. In older houses in the inner city the walls are often thick and the dwellings in terraced form; in more modern houses in the suburbs the cavity walls may be sufficiently effective without the need for filling or other additional measures. The only areas where roof insulation falls below 50 per cent are in the inner city, such as Stonehouse, and the only areas where wall insulation exceeds 20 per cent are in the owner-occupied suburbs.

Fig. 40. Households Possessing Roof and/or Wall Insulation.

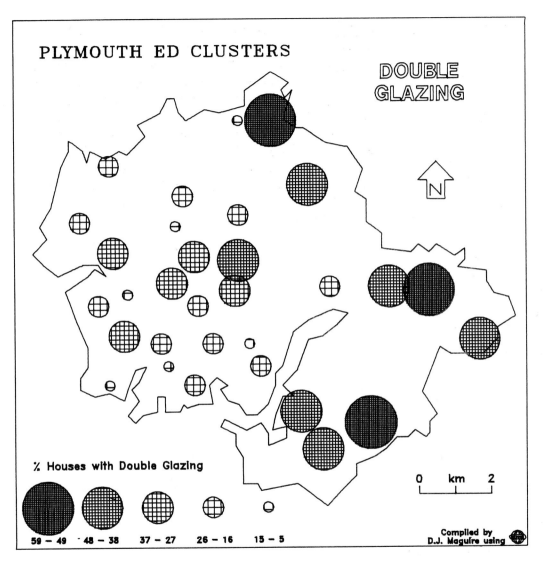

PLYMOUTH ED CLUSTERS

DOUBLE
GLAZING

N

% Houses with Double Glazing

59 – 49   48 – 38   37 – 27   26 – 16   15 – 5

0   km   2

Compiled by
D.J. Maguire using

Fig. 41. Households Possessing Double-Glazed Windows.

The 'geography of double glazing' (**Fig. 41**) shows a clear east-west division. With the exception of the Compton/Eggbuckland area, double-glazing is heavily concentrated in the eastern and north-eastern suburbs. Here it has been incorporated into new private housing and added to existing owner-occupied properties. Double glazing reduces both drafts and heating bills but the expense of installation means that it has a long 'pay-back' period. Many owner-occupiers obviously see it as a means of raising the value of their house as well as a device to cut heating bills. It is interesting, however, that private landlords do not seem to share this approach and there is therefore very little double-glazing in the private-rented sector. Tenants are obviously reluctant to install it because they are unlikely to stay long enough to make the investment worthwhile and because it is the landlord who would benefit from the increased property value. Landlords, on the other hand, may feel reluctant to install double-glazing or other insulation measures because it is the tenants' fuel bills and comfort levels that would improve. Clearly, this division of responsibility can be a serious impediment to home improvement.

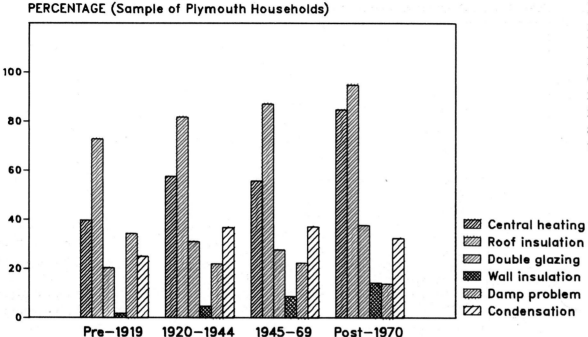

PERCENTAGE (Sample of Plymouth Households)

Central heating
Roof insulation
Double glazing
Wall insulation
Damp problem
Condensation

**Fig. 42. Energy Conservation, Heating and Damp Problems
in Dwellings of Different Age.**

Fig. 42 shows that although both central heating and roof insulation are especially common in post-1970 homes, they have also been installed in significant numbers of older dwellings. Structural damp shows a clear downward trend being least prevalent in the most modern buildings. However, there is no such improvement in the case of condensation which actually affects a higher percentage of post-1919 dwellings than those built pre-1919.

The elderly have an increased physiological need for warmth and spend a greater proportion of their time at home. It is therefore doubly important that their dwellings should be well-heated and well-insulated. However **Fig. 43** indicates that in fact the elderly occupy dwellings with rather below average levels of heating and insulation. This disturbing pattern has several possible causes including poverty and a reluctance to face the upheaval of installing new heating and insulation equipment. It is also significant that large numbers of the elderly live in older accommodation in the private-rented sector and this is a form of tenure which generally offers inferior standards.

There are various government measures which can help pensioners and other potentially disadvantaged groups with their heating bills. There is also locally a non-profit-making body called 'The Plymouth Community Insulation Project' which helps to install insulation for pensioners, single parent families, the disabled and those receiving Supplementary Benefit.

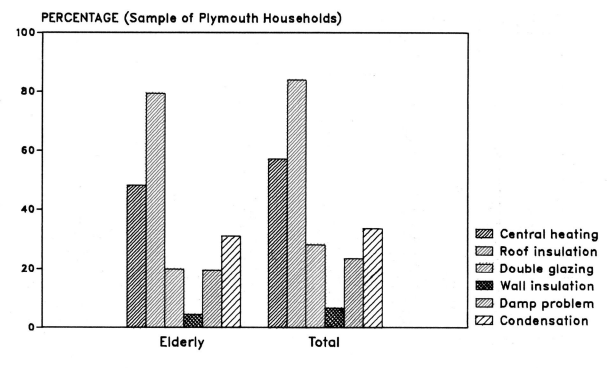

Fig. 43. Energy Conservation, Heating and Damp Problems in the Dwellings of the Elderly Population.

Housing Satisfaction

A home is more than a shelter from the elements and an assemblage of amenities. It is a base for family life, a place for leisure and pleasure and a symbol of one's social status: it also represents a sizeable part of most families' total expenditure and for owner-occupiers it is commonly their most financially valuable possession. For these reasons, the physical measures of housing amenities reviewed in earlier sections provide a useful but only partial view of the quality of housing which people actually perceive and experience. For example, living at more than 1.5 persons per room may be quite intolerable under certain conditions, but acceptable under others: much depends on the individuals involved.

In order to probe therefore beyond the physical characteristics of the dwelling stock, the household survey sought to assess housing quality by asking people how they felt about their accommodation. The replies indicated a generally very high level of contentment. Overall, 65 per cent said they were very satisfied, 29 per cent were reasonably satisfied and only six per cent were to some degree dissatisfied. These results would seem strongly to reinforce the view of Plymouth as a city with mercifully few serious housing problems. However, a word of caution is needed. Contentment can be the product of acceptance and endurance rather than genuine comfort and pleasure. Moreover, some of those interviewed may have been unwilling to admit to disagreeable housing conditions seeing this as a mark of personal failure. Nonetheless, despite these reservations, the clear impression remains of a city whose people generally feel themselves to be well-housed.

Fig. 44 shows that a high level of satisfaction is found in all parts of the city and in none of the study areas did the proportion "very satisfied" fall below 50 per cent. Although the survey did not cover all of the city's less-prosperous areas (for example, the Prince Rock and Cattedown areas to the east of Sutton Pool, were not examined) there is no reason to suppose that the inclusion of different sample areas would have radically altered the general pattern of the results.

Even in the inner city and on the older council estates, the majority of those interviewed expressed themselves well-pleased with their housing conditions. Nonetheless, as expected, the highest levels of satisfaction were generally found in the eastern suburbs and in the Compton and Peverell areas close to Mannamead. The highest proportion of those dissatisfied (16 per cent) was found in the North Prospect/Ford area, though this figure was only marginally above that for several other parts of western and inner Plymouth. Among dissatisfied households the most common problems were the dwelling's poor state of repair and small size. Relatively few complained that their accommodation was too large which suggests that under-occupation is not a widespread or common problem. Similarly, there were few complaints about housing cost: presumably few people stay long in dwellings they cannot afford.

Finally, it is of interest that the level of spatial contrast in perceived housing quality, as revealed in our survey (Fig. 44), is rather less than might have been expected from a general knowledge of the city and the very noticeable differences between its constituent neighbourhoods. This points to opinions, especially in the less-prosperous areas, being conditioned by what people felt they could reasonably aspire to. Housing conditions which would have been regarded as wholly unsatisfactory in Compton and Plymstock were viewed as quite acceptable in Mutley and Keyham.

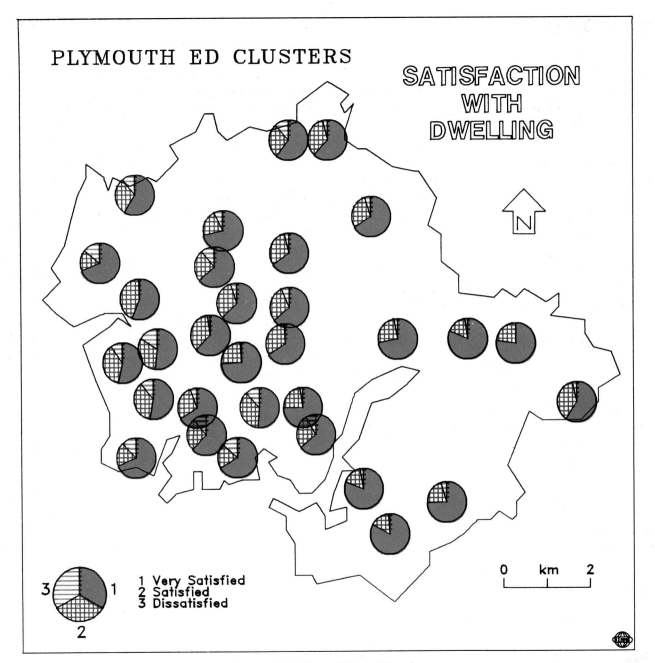

Fig. 44. Levels of Satisfaction with Dwelling: By Area.

The Assessment of Housing: The Local Authority Approach

Having outlined the appraisal of the housing stock by its occupants, the discussion now moves on to consider how the local authority tackles the problem of housing assessment. In the Local Plan Report of Survey (1980) the city's planners used Census and other data to forecast future housing requirements. Their calculations took into account both the size and quality of the existing dwelling stock and predicted future needs based on demographic forecasts. They estimated, for example, that by 1991 a further 13,900 dwellings would be needed.

In addition to the planners' long-term estimates of future housing need, the city's Environmental Health Department is engaged in assessing present-day housing conditions and trying to enforce certain basic standards as set out in the 1985 Housing Act. Judgements are made about what work, if any, needs to be undertaken to bring dwellings up to the required standard. Over the years the standards expected have risen and since 1980 the occupants' personal comfort has to be taken fully into account as well as matters of safety and hygiene. The local authority has the power to insist that the necessary building work is undertaken and, in extreme cases, is permitted to do the work itself and bill the landlord later.

A third local-authority department closely involved with dwelling standards is, of course, the city Housing Department: this is responsible primarily for the repair, management and allocation of Plymouth's 22,642 council dwellings. In order to allocate vacancies in this housing stock to households in greatest need, the local authority has devised a set of procedures known as the "points system". This system is of special interest in that it has a direct bearing on the housing opportunities of thousands of people in the city. For this reason it is outlined below, although of course anyone wanting council accommodation should obtain further details direct from the local authority.

For every applicant household the city council assesses the size of dwelling required. Points are then awarded (see the table opposite) according to the extent to which the applicant's present accommodation falls below the required size. In addition, points are awarded for a lack of basic amenities such as a bathroom or inside WC. Applicants are not awarded points until 12 months after registering with the local authority, during which time they must have been living within the city. A somewhat similar points system operates for council tenants wanting a transfer. In this case, extra points are given to tenants of flats, maisonettes and pre-war council houses: this provides an opportunity for upward mobility within the council sector. Households with the most points are normally given the first chance of any appropriate vacancies in areas they consider suitable. At present families looking for two, three or four bedroomed accommodation would normally need over 80 points to obtain an offer (the exact figure would depend on their area(s) of preference). For one bedroom accommodation, the current score is about 30 points.

Before 1980 applicants were graded on their housekeeping standards in order to determine the quality of dwelling for which they would be a suitable tenant. (This procedure has now been substantially amended though not entirely discarded). Allocating the best houses to the "best" applicants protected the most valuable modern dwellings from the misdemeanours of uncaring tenants. However, this system (which was common in other cities too) may have inadvertently contributed to the creation of "problem" estates with high proportions of difficult tenants. Although preliminary enquiries by the local authority suggest that grading has not been a major factor in fomenting the social unrest on the North Prospect estate, the impact of grading on the city's overall social geography remains unclear. It is beyond dispute, however, that a citywide perception of Plymouth's neighbourhoods (both council and private) has developed whereby some areas are regarded as considerably more desirable than others. This informal neighbourhood grading undoubtedly shapes the attitudes of residents to their own localities and may be in part responsible for the variation in levels of satisfaction expressed by those residing in different parts of the city.

Plymouth City Council's Housing Points Scheme

(A) It is reckoned that depending on size families should have the following rooms and basic amenities.

Single persons	Bedsit, kitchen	2 rooms.
Childless couples	Bedroom, living room, kitchen	3 rooms.
Couple & 1 child or 2 children of same sex	2 bedrooms, living room, kitchen	4 rooms.
Couple & 2 children of opposite sex	3 bedrooms, living room, kitchen	5 rooms.

etc.

Points award for any shortfall of this scale:-

| Each room short | .... | 20 pts |
| Each room shared | .... | 10 pts |

(B) Additional points awarded for persons without a bedroom as follows:-

Under 4 years of age	....	20 pts
4 - 6 years	....	40 pts
7 years and above	....	60 pts

(C) Points are also awarded for lack of basic amenities:-

(a)	Sink without hot water	....	5
(b)	No sink	....	10
(c)	Carrying water or cooked food to different floor	....	5
(d)	No bathroom	....	12
(e)	Shared bathroom	....	5
(f)	Bathroom without hot water	....	5
(g)	External W.C. only	....	10
(h)	Shared external W.C.	....	12
(i)	Shared internal W.C.	....	5
(j)	Difficult access to accommodation	....	5
(k)	Substandard accommodation e.g. poor state of repair etc. (discretionary)	....	0-15
(l)	Lack of clothes drying facilities (families with infants or school children)	....	5

(D) Applicants needing 1 bedroom accommodation with a points award of 30 or those needing 2 bedrooms or more with 20 pts are awarded a further 5 pts for each year from the date the points award became valid.

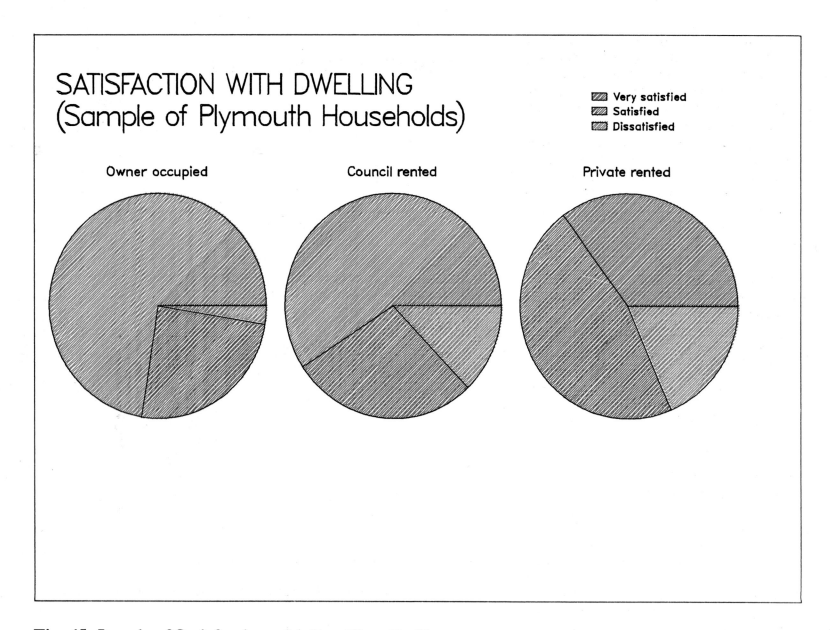

SATISFACTION WITH DWELLING
(Sample of Plymouth Households)

Very satisfied
Satisfied
Dissatisfied

Owner occupied

Council rented

Private rented

Fig. 45. Levels of Satisfaction with Dwelling: By Tenure.

In continuing the theme of housing appraisal, **Fig. 45** shows the extent to which people's assessment of their dwelling varies according to tenure. The proportion dissatisfied is at its lowest, three per cent, among owner-occupiers, rises to 13 per cent among council tenants, and peaks at 19 per cent among tenants in the private-rented sector. Owner-occupied housing is generally well-provided with basic amenities and kept in good repair by its owners most of whom will have chosen the property because it meets their needs. Most council accommodation is also physically of a good standard but, with tenants having comparatively little choice of dwelling, it is not surprising that satisfaction levels are somewhat lower. Private-rented dwellings are the least well-provided with basic amenities, are in the poorest state of repair and also suffer from conflicts between landlord and tenant. Nonetheless, even in this sector the majority of households were satisfied with their accommodation, though some of the transient members of the inner city population may have been prepared to look favourably on short-term living conditions which would not have been acceptable over a longer period. For many the private-rented sector is not so much a destination as a waiting room and as such its occupants may be less critical of its deficiences.

When considering housing quality it is important to take into account not only people's perceptions of their individual dwellings but also their views on the neighbourhoods in which their dwellings are located. The household survey revealed that overall 71 per cent of households were very satisfied with their local neighbourhood and a further 21 per cent reasonably satisfied. As expected **Fig. 46** shows that discontentment was largely confined to the western and inner city areas. Perhaps more surprisingly, however, people's complaints were directed less at the local environment and its facilities than at their neighbours and the lifestyles and behaviour of the people who shared the local area.

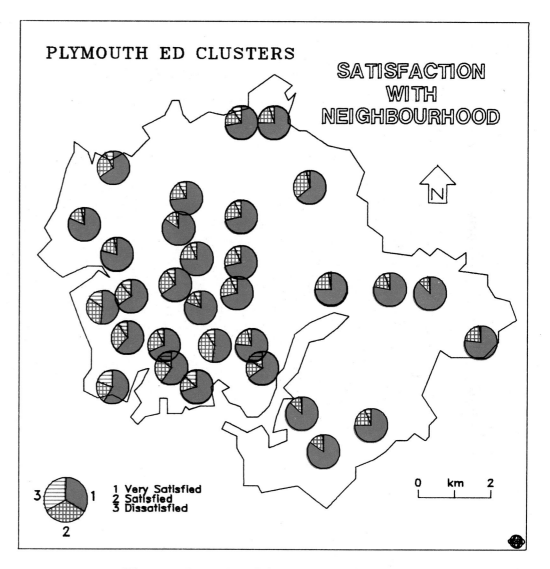

Fig. 46. Levels of Satisfaction with Neighbourhood.

Residential Preferences

Where people actually live is only a very imperfect guide to where they would ideally like to live. For all kinds of reasons, but principally insufficient money, most people are unable to obtain accommodation in the area they would select if given an entirely free choice. In order therefore to reveal the geography of residential preference, the household survey asked the question, "If money were no object, and you could choose to live anywhere in the Plymouth area, where would you most like to live?"

The "top ten" areas, as identified in **Fig. 47,** shows two very clear patterns. The first is the dominance of Plymstock and Plympton. These eastern suburbs were only incorporated into the city following the 1967 boundary extension, but they have, on this evidence, already become Plymouth's most desirable areas. Being recent additions to Plymouth they are largely free from council housing and are characterised by generally pleasant, if architecturally undistinguished, semi-detached houses. Both have local shopping centres and schools with good reputations. Both offer to some extent the social advantages of "small town life" in that being geographically somewhat separate from the rest of Plymouth they enjoy a degree of identity and community less easily achieved in other suburbs. Plymstock is the more favoured of the two, perhaps because it has less industry, a more varied housing stock, and rather quicker access to the city centre. A recent survey by Oats Partridge, one of the city's leading estate agents, showed average house prices to be £45,086 in Plymstock compared with £40,945 in Plympton.

The second main feature of Fig. 47 is the line of preference stretching northwards from The Hoe through Mannamead and Crownhill to the city boundary at Roborough. North of the city centre this line follows, in part, a ridge of higher ground leading up to the southern slopes of Dartmoor (see topographic map, Fig. 6).

That only five per cent singled out The Hoe as their most preferred area is in some ways a surprisingly low figure: the panoramic views and proximity to the city centre make this in fact a much sought-after area. However, it contains only a very limited stock of private dwellings and perhaps for this reason few of our respondents considered it as a possible area of residence.

Mannamead was nominated by six per cent of those interviewed. It is without doubt the main high-status area of Plymouth and it enjoys considerable social prestige. The large villas and handsome Victorian family houses offer an attractive environment which is within easy reach of the city centre, the shopping parade at Mutley Plain, and a number of private schools. Some interviewees may have declined to nominate Mannamead for fear of seeming "posh" or having ambitions beyond their station. That it did not attract a higher vote may also reflect a feeling that Mannamead is in danger of encroachment from the flats and bed-sits on its southern borders. Its status as a Conservation Area should help avert this danger but there are considerable pressures for nursing and old people's homes and for high quality flats which might in time alter the character of the area.

As expected, the western side of Plymouth, with its combination of Victorian terraces and council houses, attracted very little support. The only exception was Stoke. Here there is a local shopping centre and a stock of older, elegant buildings, including some designed by Plymouth's most famous architect, John Foulston. Stoke also enjoys a reputation for a good local community life; indeed the central area is often referred to as "Stoke Village".

The major zone of predominantly private housing to exert very little appeal lies in north-eastern Plymouth between Crownhill and Plympton. Here in areas such as Estover, Leigham, Mainstone and Thornbury are substantial recently-built estates. However, many of them are architecturally uninspired and there are insufficient shopping and other local facilities. The area lacks a proper centre. Indeed, much the same can be said of the entire northern half of the city. There are small local shopping parades, as at Crownhill, but many of these northern suburbs, four or so miles from the city centre, lack an adequate range of facilities and services. There are now planning policies which are intended in time to ameliorate this problem but until they come to fruition, few parts of northern Plymouth are likely to enjoy the popularity of Plymstock and Plympton.

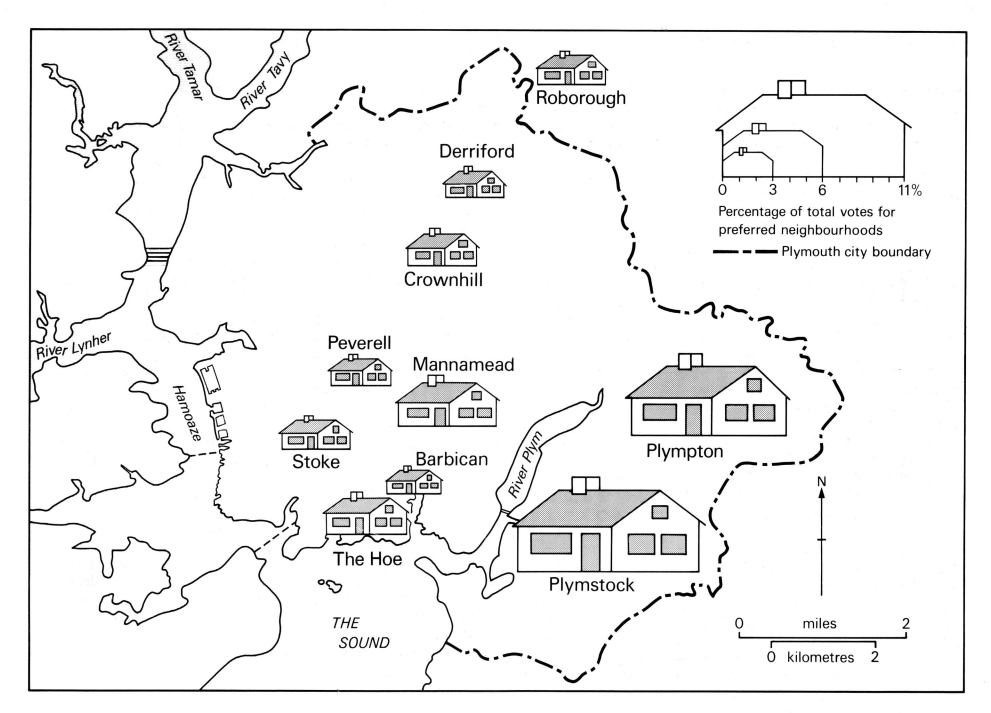

Fig. 47. Residential Preferences: Plymouth's Favoured Areas.

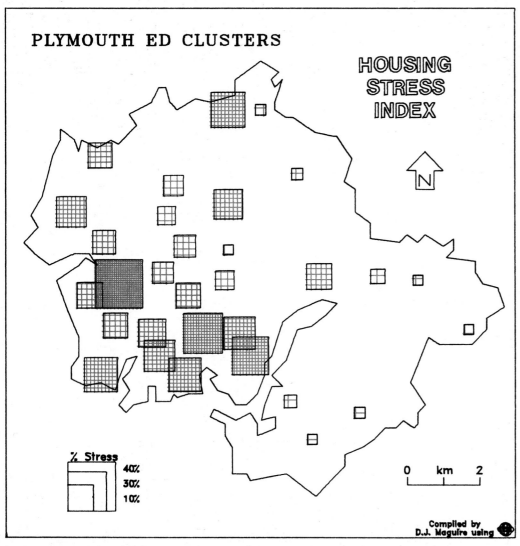

PLYMOUTH ED CLUSTERS

HOUSING
STRESS
INDEX

N

% Stress
40%
30%
10%

0   km   2

Compiled by
D.J. Maguire using

Fig. 48. A Composite Index of Housing Stress.

This final map in the housing conditions chapter provides a
synoptic view of the geography of housing stress. Whereas
each of the previous maps has looked at one particular aspect
of housing, **Fig. 48** brings together a series of individual
indicators in order to provide a more comprehensive
picture. Eleven variables, all measured in percentages, were
used to compile this index. For each area these percentage
scores were added up and then averaged. (This admittedly
rather crude procedure in effect affords equal weighting to
all variables and does not attempt to assess their relative
importance as sources of deprivation). The 11 household
variables used were:-

percentage – in dwellings built pre-1919
              – with no roof insulation
              – with no double glazing
              – with no wall insulation
              – reporting structural damp
              – reporting condensation
              – sharing rooms
              – sharing hallways, passages and landings
              – wanting to move out
              – dissatisfied with their dwelling
              – dissatisfied with their neighbourhood

The key finding to emerge from Fig. 48 is that the single
highest level of overall housing stress is in the North
Prospect/Ford area (on either side of Wolseley Road).
Although when using individual indicators of housing
quality, this area does not always stand out as the
neighbourhood with the most severe problems, when
individual measures are aggregated it becomes clearly the
most disadvantaged locality. It should be noted that the
survey data behind the map were collected well before the
1986 disorders and are not therefore a response to this
unrest. How far these survey results shed light on the
background causes of the disturbances is by no means
certain. The reader will recall that this area also suffers from
particulary high levels of unemployment (see pages 40 and
41).

Six
**Community
Issues**

Community Issues

From the potentially wide range of community issues which could be considered, this chapter selects three themes of particular significance and interest. The first is social welfare and there are maps to show the geography of households with special needs, such as single-parent families. The second topic is crime, and maps are included which identify those areas most/least affected by various forms of criminal activity. The third and final section deals with local politics and illustrates the strong connection between how people vote and where they live.

Social Welfare: Households with Special Needs

Any discussion of welfare or deprivation is inevitably beset by the problem of how it should be measured. On some indicators, Plymouth fares better than the national norm and, on others, worse. Overall, there are grounds for believing that the people of Plymouth enjoy a quality of life which is at least no worse than the UK average and may perhaps be somewhat better. Previous chapters have shown, for example, that for most local households housing conditions are broadly satisfactory. In particular, the tower blocks and deck access complexes which have given rise to such serious social problems in other cities have not left their mark here. Plymothians also benefit from the city's environmental attractions, its clean air, its modern facilities and its geographical setting between moor and sea. In assessing levels of social well-being it is also significant that the ethnic minorities form such a small proportion of the city's population (only 1.6 per cent were born in the New Commonwealth or Pakistan). Since Britain's black populations suffer disproportionately from various forms of deprivation and disadvantage, their near-absence in Plymouth has the effect of statistically lifting the city's average level of well-being.

It is no doubt for these kinds of reasons that Plymouth has received so little government aid from programmes aimed at relieving urban deprivation. The spate of national measures to combat inner-urban decay has by-passed Plymouth. The city has no Enterprise Zone, no Industrial Improvement Area, no Housing Action Area and has recently lost its entitlement to bid for funds from the government's Urban Programme.

Although when viewed from Whitehall, the city's problems may seem modest and remote, there are in fact some grounds for concern. Unemployment is above the national figure and incomes below it. The non-professional classes (those most at risk from poverty and social disadvantage) form an above-average proportion of the city's population. These groups are also most at risk from health problems and yet on many measures of health expenditure Plymouth is less well-resourced than the national average. Moreover, Plymouth's new hospital on the city's northern edge at Derriford is remote from many of the areas of greatest social and medical need in the inner city and Devonport.

The city's social problems as expressed in unemployment, poverty, poor health and family difficulties are often inter-related and compounded by their concentration in the areas of least-desirable housing either in the private-rented sector of the inner city or in the older council estates. Although some individuals in these areas will suffer from several different forms of disadvantage ("multiple deprivation") it would be wrong to suppose that all or even the majority of residents in such areas are seriously deprived. Equally, one should not ignore the plight of individuals and families with problems living in other parts of the city. In practice, the overall mosaic of disadvantage is intricate and the maps in this and previous chapters can portray only the broad outlines.

The task of dealing with the city's social and family problems falls principally on the County Council's Social Services Department. This is based at Exeter, but there are local offices in Plymouth. The Social Services Department obviously seeks to assist with the problems of people in all social groups, and wherever in the city they happen to reside. In practice, however, certain kinds of households are more likely to need support. The geographical distribution of some of the groups most at risk is portrayed in the maps which follow.

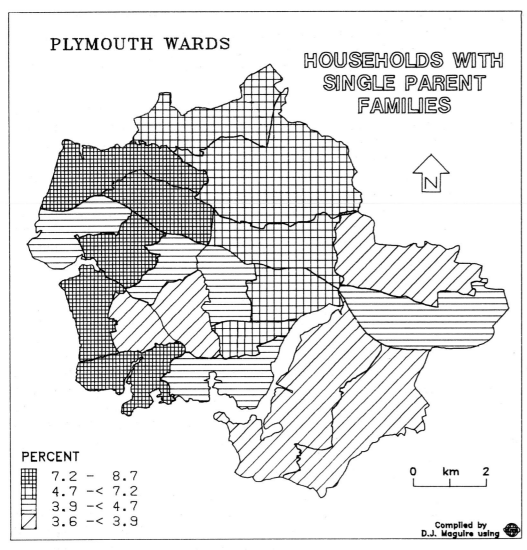

PLYMOUTH WARDS

HOUSEHOLDS WITH SINGLE PARENT FAMILIES

N

PERCENT

▦	7.2 — 8.7
▦	4.7 −< 7.2
▤	3.9 −< 4.7
▨	3.6 −< 3.9

0   km   2

Compiled by
D.J. Maguire using

Fig. 49. Households with Single-Parent Families.

Single parents are obviously prone to special difficulties and pressures. Bringing up children without a partner can be very demanding, particularly if the lone parent has to work full-time. Single-parent families can take a variety of forms: some, for example, are unmarried mothers, others are on their own because their spouse has died or, more commonly, because of marital breakdown. In Plymouth at the time of the 1981 Census, there were 4,771 single parents with one or more children under the age of 16 (about 5 per cent of all households). Of these, 2,114 were living alone and the others were part of larger households. Many one-parent families need special support particularly if, with the loosening of extended family ties, there are no local relatives available or willing to help.

Within Plymouth the highest proportion of households containing a lone parent responsible for at least one dependent child is in Ham (8.7 per cent) and the lowest is in Drake (3.6 per cent). **Fig. 49** shows that generally it is the north-west suburbs and south-west parts of the inner city which have the highest concentrations. Both areas have large stocks of council dwellings (houses in the suburbs and flats in the inner city) and it is significant that at present over one-third of those on the local authority priority housing list are one-parent families. The spatial patterns revealed in Fig. 49 may well in part, therefore, reflect the role of local authority housing provision in meeting the needs of single parents. Other relevant factors could include spatial variations in age structure (divorce rates are highest among young adults) and the general level of economic and social welfare. Whatever its causes, the geography of single-parent households is an important indicator of social need. Interestingly, however, in Plymouth it does not tell the full story because in practice many naval wives, with husbands away on duty, also have to operate to some degree as single parents. The presence of the Armed Forces must therefore colour any picture of the city's family life.

Although the majority of large households function well, size can bring disadvantages. These may include overcrowding, shared bedrooms, domestic pressures and for children the danger of less individual care and supervision from their parents. Within Plymouth child abuse is most common in the north-west sector and in Keyham and Devonport. These areas do face a variety of economic and social problems but it may not be entirely coincidence that they are both areas with above average proportions of large families (see **Fig. 50**). It must be borne in mind, however, that even in these areas the percentage of large households is small and in Plymouth as a whole only 3.2 per cent of households contain six or more members. Here, as elsewhere in Britain, there has been a long-term reduction in average household size.

It is noticeable that the areas with the highest proportion of large households all include substantial council estates typified by the three-bedroomed houses. It is possible therefore that council dwellings are accommodating not only a large number of single-parent families (as discussed on page 75) but also a high proportion of large households. Three-bedroomed suburban council houses are obviously better able to accommodate large households than the bed-sitters and flats (public and private) of the inner city. However, it is significant that there are very few large households in three-bedroomed private housing. The concentration of large households in areas of council housing may perhaps reflect a strategy whereby people on low incomes share dwellings as a means of keeping accommodation costs to a minimum.

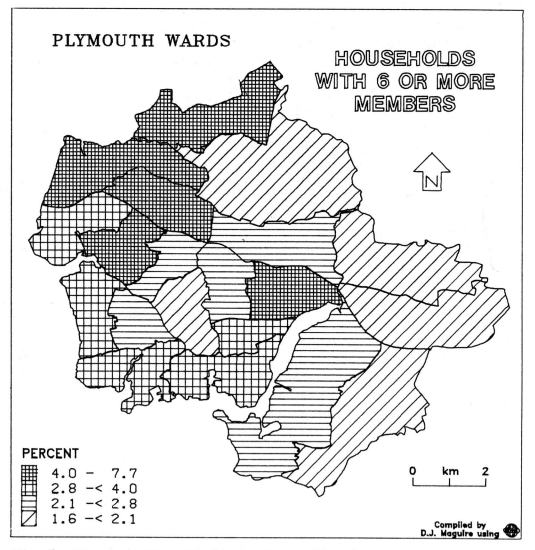

Fig. 50. Households with Six or More Members.

The 1981 Census showed that 13.2 per cent of Plymouth households comprise one old-age pensioner living alone. Of Plymouth's elderly population over a quarter (some 11,595 individuals) live by themselves. Their spatial distribution shown in **Fig. 51** is broadly similar to that of the city's elderly population as a whole (see pages 28 and 29) and there is a clear concentration in the inner city. The highest proportion is found in Drake (18.4 per cent) and the lowest in Southway (5.8 per cent). In terms of housing tenure, pensioners living alone form a below average proportion in owner-occupation (44.5 per cent as against 55.2 per cent of all Plymouth households). They are over-represented in council housing (32.1 per cent compared with the average 27.1 per cent), in the private-rented sector (17.3 per cent as against 14.7 per cent) and in housing association dwellings (5.9 per cent compared with 2.7 per cent).

Elderly people living alone can suffer not only from isolation, but they are also prone to self-neglect and, in severe cases, to physical and mental deterioration. Social Services, such as home helps, meals on wheels, and day care centres, play a key role in providing the support they require. Both social and medical provision must be carefully targeted so that the needs of old people living alone are identified and satisfied.

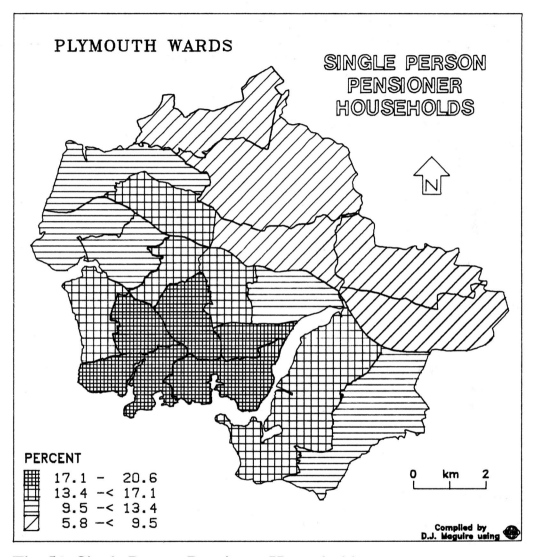

Fig. 51. Single Person Pensioner Households.

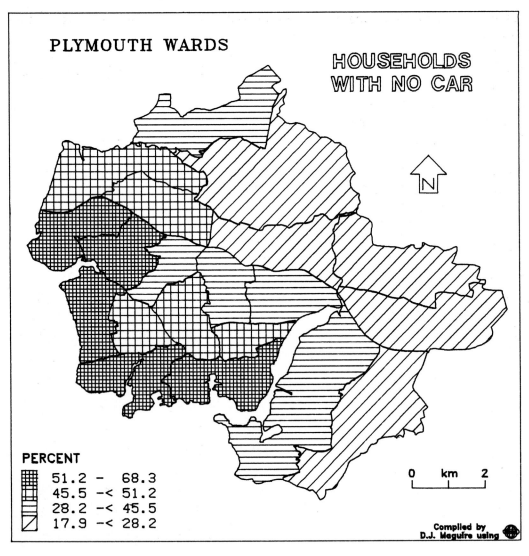

PLYMOUTH WARDS

HOUSEHOLDS WITH NO CAR

N

PERCENT
- 51.2 – 68.3
- 45.5 –< 51.2
- 28.2 –< 45.5
- 17.9 –< 28.2

0 km 2

Compiled by
D.J. Maguire using

Fig. 52. Households with No Car.

The proportion of households without a car is a widely used indicator of disadvantage both because it is a surrogate measure for income and because, in certain areas and for certain people, the absence of a car can pose serious problems of accessibility and isolation. The 1981 Census showed that in Plymouth as a whole the proportion of households with no car was 41.0 per cent, which is fractionally above the national average of 39.5 per cent. The Devon figure for no car households was 37.3 per cent which reflects the fact that in many of the rural parts of the County, the dearth of public transport makes car ownership essential.

Within Plymouth **Fig. 52** reveals that the areas of lowest car ownership form an "L" shaped band stretching from St. Budeaux southwards to St. Peter, and then eastwards across the inner city into Sutton. This very distinctive spatial pattern is in part a reflection of income levels and of age structure (many elderly people being unable to drive or to afford a car). It also derives from the fact that proximity to the city centre and the dockyard (the two main employment areas) reduces the need to own a car. In practice, some of the worst problems of accessibility are found on the northern council estates where households with no car face long journeys by public transport to the main centres of employment and shopping.

Crime in Plymouth

Although in many respects Plymouth is geographically still a somewhat isolated city, it has not been immune from the national trend towards increasing levels of crime. Of course, by the standards of the nation's conurbations Plymouth's problems remain relatively modest, yet for the Devon and Cornwall Constabulary Plymouth is much the largest centre of criminal activity with 27 per cent of the region's recorded crime (as against 18 per cent of its population). The accompanying table provides a detailed breakdown of crime in the Plymouth area and points to a 46 per cent increase in offences between 1981 and 1985. This figure is somewhat inflated by the inclusion in the post-1983 statistics of adjacent areas of West Devon, but since these add only 11 per cent to the Plymouth total the rising tide of local crime is clearly evident.

Apart from general theft, the table highlights house burglary and theft from and of motor vehicles as among the most numerous crimes. Data on both of these and on general assault are shown in map form in **Figs. 53, 54** and **55**. The maps are based on 1984 information, the last year for which the appropriate data were available. For a variety of technical reasons, a degree of caution is needed when interpreting crime statistics (and maps which use them) not least because of the unquantifiable difference between the number of crimes reported to the police and the number actually committed. Small spatial or temporal variations in the official statistics may not be significant: nonetheless, it is known that the major geographical patterns considered below are consistent over time and of enduring importance. Do note, however, that the maps show the total number of offences rather than the rates per 1,000 residents (this is because the police unit areas do not coincide with the spatial units adopted in the Population Census). But although the generally higher crime levels in the city's central areas are therefore partly the product of the higher residential densities, this is by no means a sufficient explanation. The four square miles of central Plymouth contain less than 15 per cent of the city's population and over 50 per cent of its total recorded crime.

Crime in Plymouth and Adjacent Parts of West Devon: 1981 - 1985

	1981*	1984	1985	%increase 1981-1985*
Serious violence including homicide	14	31	32	129
General assault	463	513	513	29
Indecency	109	162	172	58
House burglary	1487	2267	2170	46
Shop burglary	459	603	574	25
Office burglary	276	274	317	15
School burglary	227	283	252	11
Other burglary	462	498	575	24
Robbery including 'mugging' handbag snatching etc.	89	119	142	60
Theft from vehicles	1597	2078	2419	51
Theft of vehicles	1619	1794	1614	−0.03
Theft from shops	1361	1582	1753	29
Theft from meters	250	482	597	139
General theft	2446	3505	3711	52
Fraud, Forgery	376	1081	1089	190
Criminal damage (vandalism)	861	1302	1433	66
Other crime	194	417	461	138
Totals	12290	17091	17908	46

* The 1981 figures do not include Plympton, Plymstock, Tavistock and Ivybridge which together are currently responsible for about 11 per cent of the area's total crime. (Data from the Devon and Cornwall Constabulary Crime Prevention Support Unit at Crownhill, Plymouth).

Fig. 53 reveals that the victims of residential burglary are mainly to be found in the inner city areas such as Devonport and Keyham and in the older council estates such as Efford. In the inner areas, the larger numbers of flats and multi-occupied dwellings provide easier and more abundant opportunities for burglary and especially for crimes such as meter thefts. The older council estates are also at risk because, paradoxically, it is usually a city's poorer areas (and those with the worst unemployment) which show the highest incidence of burglary. It is noticeable that Plympton and Plymstock, which together form the city's largest area of owner-occupied housing, have by far the lowest burglary figures. This may in part reflect a higher degree of security-consciousness amongst people who own their own homes and who can afford to pay for locks, fittings and other devices to deter the criminal.

It is important to stress that the map shows where burglars operate, not where they live. Of course, residential burglaries (and especially minor thefts) are often opportunistic crimes rather than carefully planned or premeditated: for this reason a proportion of offenders may indeed live nearby or in adjacent areas. However, further research would be needed before any definitive statements could be made on this inevitably sensitive issue. Fig. 53 should be used therefore only to identify the geography of the victims of crime and not its perpetrators. Similarly, although the Devonport area shows both high levels of crime and of unemployment (see pages 40 and 41) this should not be taken as definitive proof of a connection between the two.

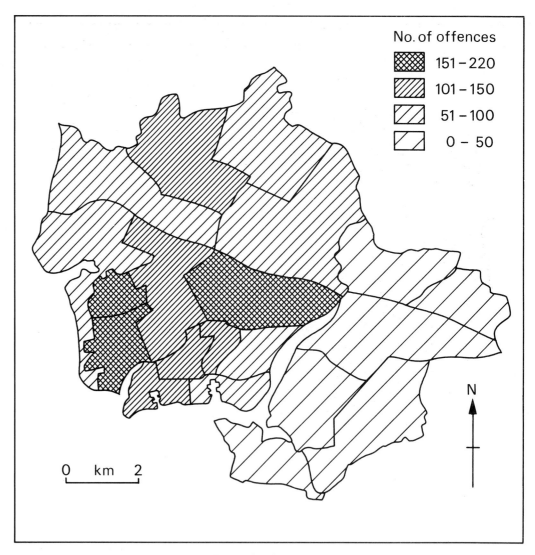

No. of offences

151–220

101–150

51–100

0 – 50

0   km   2

N

Fig. 53. Reported House Burglaries.

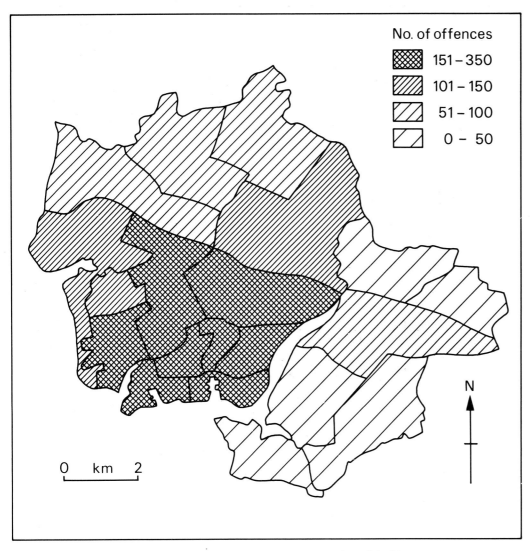

No. of offences

151 – 350	
101 – 150	
51 – 100	
0 – 50	

0   km   2

N

Fig. 54. Reported Theft of or from Motor Vehicles.

The marked concentration of thefts of or from vehicles (**Fig. 54**) in the central parts of the city obviously reflects the higher densities of parked vehicles. The multi-storey car parks in and adjacent to the main shopping centre are particularly at risk and discussions have taken place between the police and the local authority engineers to ensure that the design of any future multi-storey car parks in the city takes full account of surveillance and security needs. More immediately a campaign has been launched to alert the Plymouth public to the threat of thefts from cars which rose particularly sharply in 1986, at a rate well above the national average. The increase in the theft of credit cards from cars is especially worrying in that this invariably leads on to a series of further offences.

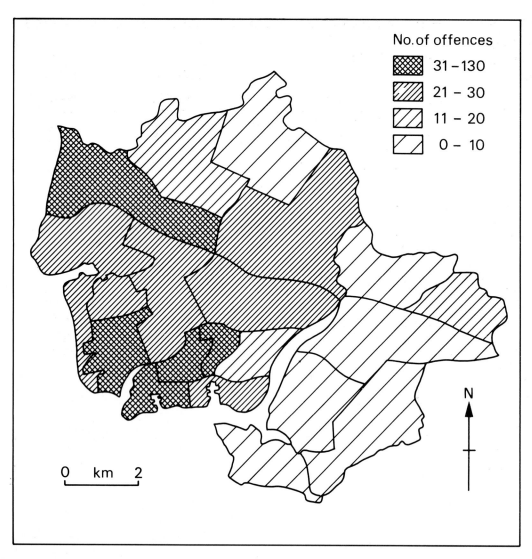

No. of offences

31 – 130
21 – 30
11 – 20
0 – 10

0   km   2

N

Fig. 55. Reported Assaults.

The crimes included in **Fig. 55** are those which cause "actual bodily harm" (such as woundings, broken limbs and black eyes) but which stop short of murder. By far the highest figures are those for the area around Union Street, the city's main concentration of nightclubs, which is on the western perimeter of the city centre. Relatively few assaults take place within the clubs themselves but the streets around are the most dangerous in Plymouth. Other parts of the inner city, as in Devonport, Stoke and Drake, also experience above average levels of assault though their figures fall well below those for Union Street. The inclusion of the Ernesettle – Whitleigh area (with its large council estates) in the top category is perhaps best regarded as a statistical anomaly in that its assault figure only narrowly qualified for this group. In practice, most of the city's areas with large council estates fall into the second tier, leaving the middle-class owner-occupied areas with the lowest figures. (The apparently rather high figure for Mannamead may result from it being in the same police unit area as Efford). Plympton and Plymstock form by far the largest "low assault" zone and it is noticeable how on all three of the offence maps these two eastern suburbs consistently emerge as low crime areas. Plympton and Plymstock were identified in Chapter Five as the city's most desirable residential areas: one can only presume that if the facts of crime geography were better known the popularity of eastern Plymouth would be still more pronounced.

Politics and Voting Patterns

Politically, Plymouth is an anomoly. On the basis of its social class composition one would expect a strong Labour vote. In practice, the city council has been in Conservative control for over 20 years and none of the three parliamentary constituencies has a Labour MP. Plymouth may therefore be characterised as a working-class town with middle-class politics. The reasons are not hard to find. The patriotic sentiments of the dockyard workers and of the Armed Services have traditionally strengthened the Tory vote, and more recently in the Devonport constituency there is a large personal vote for David Owen, leader of the SDP.

Plymouth's three parliamentary constituencies were fought in their present form (see **Fig. 56**) for the first time in the 1983 general election, boundary changes having been so extensive that the new seats resemble the old in name only. Indeed, the campaign to save the old constituency names has led to some interesting anomolies. The Devonport constituency now occupies large areas of northern Plymouth and much of Devonport itself is no longer within the constituency, having been transferred to Drake. Moreover, the Sutton constituency no longer includes the Sutton Ward, it too having been transferred to Drake.

The tables opposite provide a brief statistical profile of the three constituencies and their voting patterns at the 1983 election. The Devonport constituency has a low proportion of professional people and a high proportion of council dwellings. The wards it comprises have traditionally voted Labour and there was much pre-election speculation about David Owen's prospects. In fact his large personal following, combined with tactical voting amongst both Labour and Tory supporters, secured a clear Alliance victory. The Drake constituency was in the mid-1970s a Tory marginal but boundary changes (including the transfer of council estates into Devonport) have made the new seat safe for the Conservatives. Its MP, Janet Fookes, is a prominent back-bencher and former chairman of the RSPCA. Sutton is by far the most middle-class of the three constituencies. Its MP, Alan Clark, is a junior minister and son of Lord Kenneth Clark, who made the celebrated BBC series on 'Civilisation'.

Plymouth's Parliamentary Constituencies: Election Results 1983

DEVONPORT

	1983 votes	% Poll
Dr. D. A. Owen (SDP)	20,843	44.4
Miss A. Widdecombe (Con)	15,907	33.9
J. Priestley (Lab)	9,845	21.0
J. E. Sullivan (Ind Con)	292	0.6
R. Bearsford-Walker (BNP)	72	0.2
Mrs F. Hill (Christian Democrat)	51	0.1
Majority	4,936	10.5

Professional and Managerial	8%	Owner-occupied	41%
Manual	53%	Council housing	46%

DRAKE

	1983 Votes	% Poll
Miss J. Fookes (Con)	19,718	50.6
W. Fitzgerald (SDP)	11,133	28.6
Ms S. Creswell (Lab)	7,921	20.3
C. W. Bradbury (BNP)	163	0.4
Majority	8,585	22.0

Professional and Managerial	15%	Owner-occupied	53%
Manual	42%	Council housing	19%

SUTTON

	1983 Votes	% Poll
A. K. M. Clark (Con)	25,203	55.1
A. Puttick (Lib)	13,516	29.6
Ms F. Holland (Lab)	6,538	14.3
S. Shaw (Ecology)	470	1.0
Majority	11,687	25.6

Professional and Managerial	17%	Owner-occupied	71%
Manual	41%	Council housing	14%

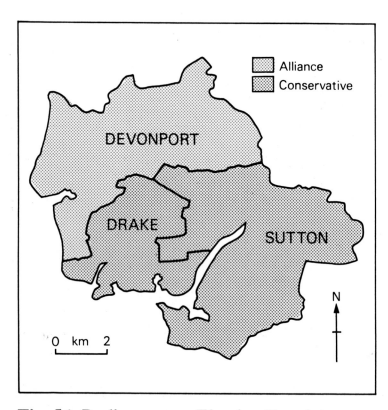

Fig. 56. Parliamentary Election Results: Plymouth 1983.

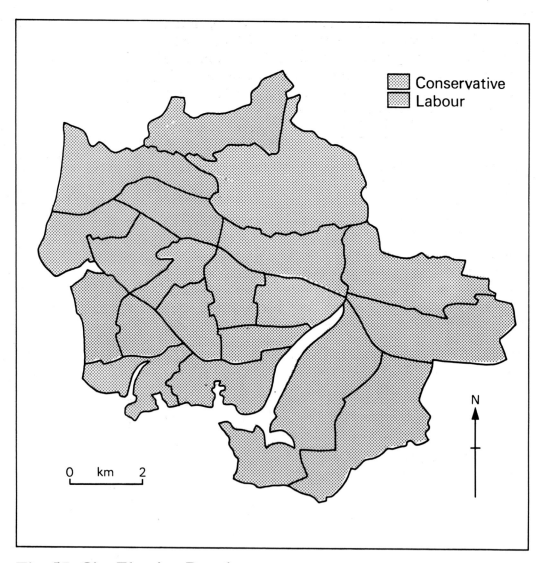

Fig. 57. City Election Results: Plymouth 1983.

Figs. 57 and 58 reveal an interesting story of political change. The city council elections in May 1983 produced a strong Conservative performance with Labour confined to parts of the inner city and the council estates of the north west. The SDP/Liberal Alliance won not a single seat. It is quite remarkable therefore that only a few weeks later in the general election David Owen should have won the Devonport constituency.

Equally remarkable is the contrast between the expected, post-Falklands, Tory victories in the city council election of 1983 and the generally unexpected Alliance victories in the county council election of 1985. The county elections (one councillor per ward) show the more middle-class areas turning strongly to the Alliance, with the Tories holding on only in Plymstock Radford. That this was the only city ward to produce a Tory majority is a measure of how much the government's threat to the dockyard has harmed Tory loyalties. However, the Alliance landslide did not make large-scale in-roads into Labour territory. It is of particular significance that many wards in David Owen's Devonport constituency voted Labour even at the time of this major swing to the Alliance. His general election victory therefore looks all the more remarkable. By the standards of the 1985 results the Devonport constituency is by far the Alliance's least-promising territory and, on this basis at least, Owen would be better placed in Sutton or Drake. Plymouth's political geography seems as perverse as it is unpredictable.

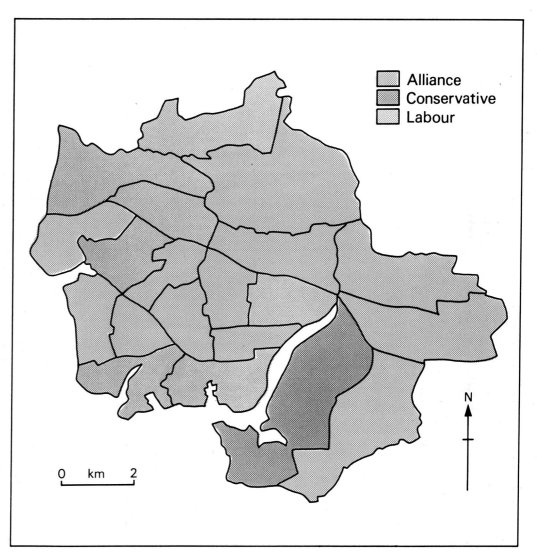

Fig. 58. Plymouth's Voting Patterns in the County Elections of 1985.

Technical Appendix

The maps and graphs in this atlas are derived from a variety of sources (see Acknowledgements, p2), the most important of which are the 1981 Population Census and the MSC household survey.

The 1981 Population Census Maps

The decennial Census of Population of Great Britain provides an unrivalled data source for the academic and the planner. For the former it represents the most comprehensive source of data readily available at a small scale, on demographic, social and economic conditions. For the latter it provides an indication of the social and economic problems which need to be tackled and where resources need to be directed. The 1981 Population Census was taken on the 5th April 1981. From each of the 54 million individuals in Britain came eight to fifteen primary answers; added to these were a further six answers relating to each household. This information, which amounts to 4,400 statistical counts for each of the 130,000 enumeration districts in Britain is summarized in published pages of tables in paper and computer form. These enumeration districts typically comprise about 200 households and are the smallest areal units for which data are published.

A copy of the 1981 Population Census data for Cornwall and Devon is held on Plymouth Polytechnic's PRIME 9950 minicomputer. The data may be accessed using the Small Area Statistics Package (SASPAC). This allows the user to extract subsets of the data (certain variables for certain areas) and to perform statistical calculations. The majority of the Census maps in this atlas depict information at ward level. These maps show the percentages of particular groups within the population of each ward. Thus the map of the population aged 0-14 (Figure 14) shows for each ward the number of people aged 0-14 inclusive, divided by the ward's total number of people. The SASPAC cell numbers on which ratios are based and the actual percentages mapped are shown in the tables at the end of the Technical Appendix. (Further details on the Census and Census definitions can be found in Rhind, 1983, and OPCS 1981.)

The wards in each map were then classified into four equal-sized groups in order to highlight variations across Plymouth. The class boundaries are therefore defined by the quartile points which for each variable divide the range of the data into four groups each consisting of five of Plymouth's twenty wards. In simple terms these maps may be interpreted as showing those areas which are significantly lower than, slightly lower than, slightly higher than and significantly higher than the average for Plymouth as a whole. The variables mapped were selected in order to show the key aspects of Plymouth's human geography.

The Census maps and most of the MSC maps discussed in the next section were compiled and drawn using a computer. The use of computers for cartographic work provides the expert with a relatively quick, reliable and low cost means of producing high quality maps and graphs. Computer mapping involves linking a data file containing the Census ratios, extracted using SASPAC, to a geographical file containing the digitized boundaries of the areas. For the maps in this atlas this was achieved using the GIMMS (Geographical Information Mapping and Modelling System) computer package developed by Tom Waugh of the Department of Geography, Edinburgh University. Basically, the mapping procedure involves digitizing the boundaries of the areas to be mapped as pairs of XY coordinates (rather like map grid references). The computer is then instructed, via the complex code in the GIMMS package, to link these points together with straight lines. The lines thus generated are then combined into wards (the areas for which the data are to be mapped). Once the boundaries are drawn, the areas are shaded according to instructions given by the user. Further details in the form of titles, a legend, scale and north point are then added to the maps. The final maps were plotted on a CalComp 81 A3 flat bed plotter. The colour maps were plotted as individual separations for each of the required colours.

MSC Survey Maps

Although the Census contains a large volume of information, a number of key aspects of social and economic geography are not included. For this reason a specially commissioned household survey was undertaken by a team provided by the Manpower Services Commission. This survey focussed mainly on aspects of housing conditions and on people's perceptions of the quality of their dwellings. Some 3,000 households were interviewed in different parts of the city.

In planning the sampling procedures the idea of selecting addresses at random throughout the city was rejected because it would have spread the research effort too thinly and in any given locality the sample size would have been too small for meaningful results. The approach adopted was therefore to select a limited number of areas which had a high degree of internal homogeneity and which each represented a particular type of social environment. The identification of suitable areas was accomplished by using 1981 Census data for each of the city's enumeration districts, of which there are over 500. In assessing each district's social character a range of variables was used including, for example, age structure, class composition, housing tenure, housing amenities, car ownership levels and migration rates. Complex statistical techniques known as Cluster Analysis and Principal Components Analysis were then used to help identify areas of the city which would meet the necessary requirements of being individually homogeneous and, in total, representative of the full spectrum of the city's social geography. The thirty-one areas chosen, each comprising a cluster of contiguous enumeration districts, are shown in Figure 2.

Within these areas identified by the statistical clustering technique the sample of households to be interviewed was selected at random from the Electoral Register. An extensive pilot survey was undertaken in order to test the questionnaire. The MSC team were given basic training in interviewing techniques and before embarking on the survey proper they were issued with detailed instructions and written notes for guidance on how to fill in the questionnaire. As batches of interviews were completed the results were coded and fed into the Polytechnic's Prime 9950 computer. The survey data-gathering was completed in February 1985 but before initiating the next stage of statistical processing a final round of checks was conducted on the MSC data base. Questionnaires which were improperly completed or considered to be of dubious reliability were discarded in order to ensure a data set of high quality.

Statistical analysis was then undertaken using SPSS (the Statistical Package for the Social Sciences). This involved summarising and describing the significant patterns and trends in the data and identifying key relationships. Data on a number of the most interesting results were then selected out ready for computer mapping. The computer mapping procedure for the MSC data was similar in many respects to that described above for the Census data. The computer drawn maps of the Plymouth ED clusters were compiled and plotted using the GIMMS package described above. The graphs and charts were compiled and plotted using the TELL-A-GRAF package, a statistical graphics package developed by ISSCO graphics of California.

The maps of Plymouth ED clusters are essentially the same as the Census maps except that, instead of shading areas, point symbols (proportional divided circles, histograms, proportional squares etc) are drawn at the centre of each cluster. Point symbol maps have the advantage of allowing more than one variable to be shown on a single map. Thus Figure 27, which shows the spatial pattern of dwelling types, depicts this information as a divided circle at the centre of each ED cluster. A more complex form of this type of map is used to show, for example, structural damp problems (Figure 38). Here the size of the circle is proportional to the percentage of dwellings with structural damp. Each circle is also divided in proportion to the percentage of these dwellings for which structural damp is a serious or minor problem.

The first stage in drawing graphs and charts using TELL-A-GRAF is the selection of a template (type of chart required) from the template library. TELL-A-GRAF then provides the user with a series of questions about the layout of the graph/chart and the data to be plotted. The chart is then compiled and plotted on a suitable plotter such as the CalComp 81 plotter used here.

In addition to the main MSC household survey whose methods and mapping procedures have been described above, two other smaller MSC surveys were also undertaken: these were concerned with the city centre and with tourism. The city centre survey was designed to assess public opinion on the quality of the central areas's shopping facilities and environment, and thereby to shed light on the successes and failures of the post-war city centre reconstruction. Following a brief pilot study, over 500 questionnaires were completed by MSC interviewers positioned at ten different locations within the central area. Some of the key findings are presented in chapter one. The tourism survey was directed at summertime visitors to the city and dealt with questions such as where people had come from, why they had chosen to visit Plymouth and how they spent their time in the city. Again over 500 questionnaires were completed. In order to minimise the problem of identifying visitors the interviewers were positioned on the Hoe and near other visitor attractions within the central area. A number of the most significant results are summarised in chapter three.

Formal Definitions of Census Variables Mapped

(See table opposite for key to figure numbers.)

Figure Number	Definition (SASPAC Cell Numbers)
14	((C57+C64+C71) DIV C50)*100
15	((C153+C154+C155+C162+C169+C176+C183) DIV C50)*100
16	(C571 DIV C450)*100
18	(C642 DIV C50)*100
20	((C5399+C5398) DIV C4449)*100
21	((C5402+C5403) DIV C4449)*100
22	(C5404 DIV C4449)*100
29	(C1426 DIV C929)*100
30	(C1427 DIV C929*100
31	((C1429+C1430+C1431+C1432) DIV C929)*100
35	(C2224 DIV C929)*100
36	(C1079 DIV C951)*100
37	(C954 DIV C951)*100
49	((C1473+C1481) DIV C929)*100
50	(C2430 DIV C929)*100
51	((C2508+C2509+C2510+C2511) DIV C1351)*100
52	(C1171 DIV C1170)*100

Plymouth 1981 Census Data for Atlas Maps: Percentages by Ward

Ward	14	15	16	18	20	21	22	29	30	31	35	36	37	49	50	51	52
Budshead	21.20	16.33	4.10	7.57	5.07	21.50	2.42	23.94	75.12	0.77	0.02	0.07	0.24	8.33	4.60	13.00	50.81
Compton	17.36	21.70	9.10	13.03	27.54	5.71	5.46	73.46	1.09	23.00	11.66	1.24	0.50	4.28	2.41	14.55	31.58
Drake	13.56	26.34	9.91	14.53	16.31	8.45	3.65	62.60	1.81	34.88	21.16	4.50	0.95	3.64	1.98	18.43	49.08
Efford	21.80	17.25	5.21	8.25	11.11	15.40	3.79	47.65	35.16	6.23	0.88	1.85	0.46	7.22	4.37	11.90	44.46
Eggbuckland	25.61	12.53	3.38	10.34	19.95	12.24	6.80	62.45	23.86	6.49	0.02	0.14	0.52	5.15	2.59	9.47	27.87
Estover	28.47	9.42	2.35	12.65	21.77	10.89	12.50	51.27	29.18	13.01	0.16	0.19	0.08	4.85	2.07	6.26	25.81
Ham	23.86	16.16	4.72	7.38	7.73	13.87	5.07	44.71	48.76	2.75	0.43	0.91	0.80	8.69	7.73	13.03	52.22
Honicknowle	20.62	19.64	5.05	7.09	10.60	17.88	3.31	36.32	60.99	2.32	0.09	0.53	0.22	7.23	4.02	14.18	46.62
Keyham	18.70	17.43	5.13	14.58	10.07	17.90	5.82	47.70	34.04	18.02	6.76	3.91	0.94	7.35	3.77	14.07	56.29
Mount Gould	16.50	23.41	9.29	12.69	14.75	10.60	4.38	62.78	8.25	27.86	18.46	4.42	1.04	5.01	3.24	17.43	48.79
Plympton Erle	25.00	11.15	3.86	13.13	24.43	7.76	12.10	77.73	8.46	9.63	0.39	0.69	0.07	4.05	1.99	7.35	20.26
Plympton St. Mary	22.98	15.14	4.93	7.57	22.34	9.61	5.45	90.46	4.86	4.47	0.31	0.98	0.03	3.68	1.93	9.16	18.00
Plymstock Dunstone	23.74	14.70	4.23	11.85	24.57	8.11	11.55	80.57	8.88	9.47	0.42	0.27	0.10	3.90	1.58	9.75	20.62
Plymstock Radford	18.01	20.59	6.61	9.02	20.51	7.34	7.34	77.92	9.36	12.35	0.96	0.84	0.25	3.85	2.53	13.81	29.24
St. Budeaux	22.59	16.70	5.56	14.20	7.97	13.21	18.22	40.80	27.56	23.43	0.78	0.78	0.25	4.54	3.24	12.13	51.39
St. Peter	17.39	20.34	6.73	16.89	6.71	13.84	9.01	15.73	49.56	28.63	11.15	4.02	2.13	8.22	3.07	19.22	68.16
Southway	27.02	6.79	1.63	9.28	15.68	15.68	11.59	37.63	51.44	10.72	0.02	0.05	0.41	7.11	4.48	5.84	31.48
Stoke	14.93	24.56	8.98	11.81	17.47	9.84	4.22	65.23	6.97	26.74	14.39	4.44	1.24	3.90	2.68	17.57	47.36
Sutton	14.26	25.27	8.33	11.90	8.69	14.41	2.54	39.75	29.04	26.48	11.53	5.89	0.85	4.54	2.94	20.62	58.91
Trelawny	17.94	24.27	8.34	7.41	14.29	11.38	2.38	64.84	28.33	6.69	3.44	1.06	0.19	4.47	2.67	16.33	40.71
Plymouth Total	20.58	17.99	5.87	11.06	15.38	12.28	6.88	55.18	27.14	14.70	5.15	1.84	0.56	5.50	3.19	13.21	40.98

14	Population aged 0-14 years	31	Private-rented dwellings
15	Population of pensionable age	35	Households not in self-contained accommodation
16	Population aged 75 years and over	36	Households lacking a bath or inside WC
18	Distribution of migrants	37	Overcrowded households
20	Professional and semi-professional households	49	Households with single parent families
21	Semi-skilled and unskilled households	50	Households with six or more members
22	Armed services households	51	Single person pensioner households
29	Owner-occupied dwellings	52	Households with no car
30	Council-owned dwellings		

Further Reading

Brayshay M.Ed., 1983	Post-War Plymouth: Planning and reconstruction. South West Papers in Geography No. 8, Plymouth Polytechnic, Plymouth.
Dean K., 1979	A social atlas of Plymouth. The College of St Mark & St John, Plymouth.
Devon County Council, 1983	County Structure Plan First Alteration: 1981 Data Base. Planning Department, Exeter.
Gill C., 1979	Plymouth: A new history, 1603 to the present day. David & Charles, Newton Abbot.
Maguire D.J., Mingins P.S., Saunders M.N.K., Whitelegg J., 1984.	Production of a census atlas by computer. Bulletin of the Society of University Cartographers, 18, 17-24.
Maguire D.J., Mohan J.F., 1986	Devon in maps: A social and economic profile. South West Papers in Geography, Occasional Series, Plymouth Polytechnic, Plymouth.
OPCS, 1981	Census 1981, Definitions, Great Britiain. HMSO, London.
Plymouth City Council, 1980	City of Plymouth Local Plan: Report of Survey. Plymouth.
Plymouth City Council, 1984	City of Plymouth Local Plan. Plymouth.
Plymouth City Council, 1986	Tomorrow's Plymouth. Plymouth.
Rhind D.W. Ed., 1983	A Census User's Handbook. Metheun, London.
Robinson A.H., Sale R.D., Morrison J.L., Muehrcke P.C., 1984	Elements of Cartography. Fifth Edition. Wiley, New York.
Watson J. Paton., Abercormbie P., 1943	Plan for Plymouth. Plymouth City Council. Plymouth.